Fighting the Si.

Linda and Roy Cecil

Published by
Linda and Roy Cecil
21 Linchfield Road
Datchet
Berkshire, SL3 9NA

ISBN 0 9536313 0 3

Designed and produced by
Axxent Ltd
St Stephens House
Arthur Road
Windsor
Berkshire, SL4 1RY

ACKNOWLEDGEMENTS

Linda and Roy wish to thank Ovacome for their encouragement and support in the making of this book. A donation of £2.50 for each copy sold from the first print run will be made to Ovacome.

CONTENTS

Background	7
Principal characters	11
What is ovarian cancer?	17
Linda's Journal	
How things can change	23
"I think we need some help"	27
Dark days and more frustration	30
Progress at last	38
"There is no cure"	44
"We were very pleased"	49
Back to the old routine	54
Stardom and trials	57
The 'C' word	60
Full circle	63
Roy's Journal	
How things can change	67
"I think we need some help"	69
Dark days and more frustration	74
Progress at last	82
"There is no cure"	87
"We were very pleased"	93
Back to the old routine	99
Stardom and trials	107
The 'C' word	112
Full circle	118
Postscript	119

BACKGROUND

This book is first and foremost about Linda. But it also involves our family, and friends, and the medical profession, whose encouragement and support throughout Linda's illness meant so much.

The realisation that all was far from well with Linda came in distinct stages, each more dramatic and terrible than the former. Like quantum leaps. The first leap came after Linda's initial examination by a gastroenterologist. Linda and I were both ignorant of the word 'ascites' but we very soon learned a lot about it from our children's medical text books. It did not make encouraging reading but we clutched at the straw that the fluid might be indicative of a less than life-threatening condition. Such optimism was soon dispelled when, in the second leap, the consultant commented to me over the phone that the analysis of the ascitic fluid had proved 'puzzling' and that internal investigation would be needed.

The final leap, on 15 August 1997, when exploratory surgery revealed extensive abdominal tumours, took us inexorably down a route which we could not have contemplated a few months earlier. For me at least that was the low point.

From that moment, when cancer was diagnosed, we resolved not to hide anything either from each other or from anyone. Linda and I have spoken openly and candidly about her illness and I think it has made it just that bit easier to manage – at least it has for me, I'll leave Linda to state what her feelings are on that aspect. I am not quite sure though whose idea it was to record the events of 1997-8 but we are pleased we did. So much has happened that without the journal, which is reproduced in the pages that follow in this brief book, we would have lost track of what occurred and when. I should add that the account of the first three months or so were not written contemporaneously. Our decision to keep the journal was not taken until around the time that cancer was diagnosed. The way the facts and feelings are presented may therefore differ from those of the post diagnosis record. They may differ. They may not. I tried to be disciplined, keeping my journal regularly updated. Linda wrote under duress, not believing that a book about her could be of the slightest interest to anyone. Hence the different styles of our respective journals. The important thing in our view was to end up with as comprehensive account as possible. Both our journals use the same chapter headings to help the reader to compare the two perceptions.

Why though do we want such a detailed record of what was a pretty ghastly period in our lives? Would it not be better now to shut the door on this traumatic year and pretend it never happened? I think the answer to the first question is that there were so many puzzling events, particularly during the early pre-diagnosis phase, that we felt we simply had to document them so that at some future time we could review them and try to make some sense of them, to learn from them. Which leads nicely to an answer to the second question.

Some 6000 women annually are diagnosed with ovarian cancer. Most will have reached the same advanced stage as Linda before being diagnosed, as the early stages are largely without symptoms. Many though will have experienced the vague shifting pains, the indigestion, the gradual abdominal swelling that Linda suffered for several months before she was finally diagnosed and treatment could be started. We feel that by documenting Linda's observations it may improve awareness of the disease and lead to prompter diagnosis and treatment. I also believe that Linda's attitude to her illness and the way she coped with the stresses of chemotherapy and surgery could serve as an encouragement to women newly diagnosed with the disease.

Cancer – of whatever nature – remains perhaps one of the most daunting diseases we can suffer from; although degenerative diseases of both mind and body cannot rank far behind. "There is no cure," said Linda's surgeon when he first examined her. And indeed the prognosis for women with the disease is not good – fewer than one in three women survive beyond five years. In the majority of cases the disease reappears after two to three years. How should any woman – and her family and friends – approach those precious years? Should she spend each day in dread of its return? Or is it better to live life to the full and simply hope that you are one of the lucky minority who survive longer.

Linda's answer is an unreserved "Yes" to the latter and I hope by sharing this account of her problem – OUR problem – that other women may be encouraged to adopt a similar outlook.

Looking at statistics alone Linda was in a low risk group but that did not stop her getting the disease. Let's hope she can also defy the survival rate statistics.

And to end this preface on a positive note – one third is a pretty substantial minority.

Roy Cecil, 1999

PRINCIPAL CHARACTERS

The Family

Linda Linda works part time in publishing, a career she entered at the end of 1995. She loves travelling, socialising and playing badminton. She is a quiet, relaxed person who rarely complains about anything. She is amazingly tolerant of Roy's (*vide infra*) behavioural excesses.

1997 had started on a high note for Linda. She celebrated her 50th birthday in the January. Roy organised a party for her, inviting friends from over many years. This was followed by a week long Nile cruise in early February.

Things began to go sour in May when she became aware of pains in her right shoulder and ribs. She initially attributed these pains to muscular strain from playing badminton.

Her cancer was diagnosed in August 1997.

Until Linda's cancer she rarely had any form of illness bar the occasional cold.

She and Roy have been married since 1967 and Linda spent the day on which they would have celebrated their Pearl Wedding in hospital – having a gastroscopy.

Roy Roy is 54. He was made redundant by BP in 1995 after thirty years service. He is involved in some voluntary work and enjoys the freedom from regular working hours. His company pension together with Linda's earnings and investment income are more than adequate for their generally modest lifestyle – although Roy has a somewhat extravagant eye for old silver. Roy is also trying to develop his literary skills – principally fiction writing – albeit with limited success. He has also learned to cook although he lacked confidence to begin with. His methodical approach stood the family in good stead during Linda's convalescence, particularly over Christmas 1997.

Roy is a hypochondriac of many years standing but in truth is relatively healthy. Linda's cancer came as a terrible blow although by the time it was diagnosed he was not altogether surprised.

Roy is a somewhat volatile restless individual. He is a born worrier – hence the hypochondria – so coping inwardly with Linda's condition posed quite a challenge.

After thirty plus years of marriage Roy still finds Linda immensely attractive. Her illness has not diminished his desire for her.

Edward 26 year old son of Linda and Roy. He studied medicine – briefly – and then biology at Bristol University. He graduated in 1995 and has since been working full time as a landscape gardener with the intention of developing his own business in due course. He has been involved with the Scout movement for many years and is currently Scout leader in Datchet. Edward – or Ed as most people refer to him – lives with Nicola his fianceé a couple of miles away.

Helen 24 year old daughter of Linda and Roy. After graduating from University of Brighton, also in 1995, with a degree in Physiotherapy, she took a year out to travel. She spent most of the time in Australia working and travelling. She cut her itinerary by some weeks at the end as Linda's condition worsened during the summer of 1997.

Helen decided against a career in physiotherapy and is currently working in computing. She lives at home with Linda and Roy.

Linda's mum

Win is 84 and lives nearby in sheltered accommodation. Although severely disabled with arthritis she has all her marbles and is remarkably stoical about both her own and Linda's condition.

Roy's dad Viv is 87 and lives in the West Midlands. He is reasonably good health but suffers from glaucoma and the usual effects of ageing. He has become somewhat less preoccupied with his own aches and pains since Linda developed cancer.

Friends and Neighbours

So many people gave encouragement and support to us during Linda's illness that rather than running the risk of offending any we omit we have decided not to list names. It is often difficult in cases like this for people to know when or if they should ask how things are progressing for fear the news may not be good. We really did appreciate the concern that our friends expressed and we were always prepared to reveal as much or as little as people wanted to know. Roy generally acted as PR front man, partly because he never minds talking but principally because Linda found that repeatedly going through the gory details, although not particularly stressful, was rather exhausting. We would like therefore to offer a huge 'thank you' to all whose support was more important than any individual might imagine.

The Medics

Sister Lorraine Green

An 'angel' based at Princess Margaret Hospital, Windsor. Lorraine administered Linda's cocktail of cytotoxins with much tenderness and encouragement.

Dr Hilary Thomas

Consultant Oncologist specialising in ovarian cancer. At the time Linda's treatment started Hilary was Senior Lecturer at Imperial College but during 1998 she took the Chair of Oncology at University of Surrey in Guildford.

Mr Angus McIndoe

Surgeon specialising in gynaecological oncology. A New Zealander, he is based in Harley Street he operates at both the Hammersmith and Wellington Hospitals.

Dr Win Parry-Williams

Until his recent retirement senior member of Randolph Medical Centre in Datchet. A keen game fisherman.

Dr Adrian Dalton

Took over from Dr Parry-Williams as senior member of the Randolph Medical Centre team. He is the GP whom Linda saw most during the early stages of her illness.

Dr Sassoon Levi

Consultant physician and gastro-enterologist. Dr Dalton referred Linda to 'Sass' when the diagnosis of her illness proved elusive. He carried out an endoscopy and two gastroscopies on Linda as well as organising an ascitic drain and a CT scan.

Mr Anil Desai

Surgeon to whom Linda was referred by Sass Levi for exploratory surgery when his observations and tests failed to reveal the cause of her problems.

The Hospitals

Thames Nuffield Slough

Linda attended as a day patient for Dr Levi's tests and then was admitted for exploratory surgery in August 1997. Situated in very pleasant surroundings Linda almost enjoyed her stay. Staff and care were of high standard.

Wexham Park (Paragon Suite)

Linda spent one uncomfortable night here while the ascitic fluid was drained.

Princess Margaret Windsor

Most of Linda's day patient treatment – chemo, blood tests, – took place here. Pleasant surroundings and friendly staff. (See Sister Lorraine)

The Hammersmith

This is a huge hospital next door to Wormwood Scrubs Prison. It has a new cancer wing, and also the Sainsbury suite for non NHS patients. Initial consultation with Mr McIndoe, and liver function test prior to chemo took place here. Some weeks after the chemo was finished Mr McIndoe performed a laparoscopy on Linda to determine whether or not she was eligible for a trial with a new drug. She was released the same day.

The Wellington St Johns Wood

This was Linda's 'home' for eight days during and after her operation to remove cancerous material. The only draw back was distance from home but the standard of care and the environment within the hospital were extremely high.

Another Major Player

Private Health Insurance

Roy's ex-employer, BP, in common with many companies, negotiates special group rates for private medical insurance with various health care providers. Roy and Linda – and the children while eligible – joined the group scheme in the early 80s and have paid into it ever since. After Roy was made redundant in 1995 he and Linda debated whether or not to continue in such a scheme. Common sense prevailed and through the private sector Linda has been able to receive top class treatment and care throughout her illness. Since the cancer was diagnosed **all** costs have been covered.

It is perhaps fair to point out that the NHS would to an extent have provided similar treatment although the drug Taxol is still not widely available for use by the NHS. This is despite evidence from clinical trials that its use in tandem with Carbo-platin significantly improves life expectancy. It is also true to say that such treatment is unlikely to be in surroundings as pleasant as those available to the insured. Linda has little doubt that her progress has been greatly assisted by the peaceful and comfortable environments in which she spent so much time.

WHAT IS OVARIAN CANCER?

Ovarian cancer has been referred to as 'The Silent Killer'. The reason for this is that the disease often eludes detection in its early stages when there are few, if any, symptoms and most women are unaware of anything unusual.

The cancer develops in two main ways. Most usually it spreads over the surface of the peritoneum (the lining of the abdomen) and the bowel. It then spreads to the omentum (the 'fatty apron' inside the abdomen), and the surface of the liver. The other common route for the cancer to spread is via the circulation of lymph fluid from the ovaries to the lymph glands in the pelvis and to those around the aorta.

More rarely the disease may spread in the blood to the liver, lungs or brain.

The development of cancer of the ovaries is classified in four main stages.

In Stage I ovarian cancer the disease affects only one or both ovaries. Symptoms may include needing to pass urine more frequently, or constipation. Usually though such symptoms are absent and only around 15% of cases are detected at this early stage. If detected then further sampling and microscopic examination is necessary to confirm that the cancer is confined to the interior of one ovary (Stage Ia), or both ovaries (Stage Ib). In such cases, surgery to remove the ovaries is usually performed. If there is evidence of cancer on the surface of the ovary or in the abdominal fluid surgery may be supplemented by chemotherapy.

In around 10% of cases the cancer will have spread to the lining of the pelvis, and may be found around the uterus, bladder and rectum. This is classified as Stage II cancer and both surgery and chemotherapy are advisable.

Most women, around 65%, with ovarian cancer are diagnosed with the disease at Stage III. By then the cancer may have involved the peritoneum, the omentum, the surface of the bowel and the lymph glands in the pelvis and around the aorta. There may be a build up of fluid (ascites) within the abdomen leading to very obvious distension of the abdomen. Other symptoms may be indigestion, constipation, loss of appetite and general discomfort. It must be stressed that such symptoms are not uncommon and most women experiencing them do not have ovarian cancer.

Linda was found to be suffering from Stage III ovarian cancer. Her earliest symptoms were pains in her right shoulder and ribs. On one occasion she experienced acute pain below her right rib cage which prompted investigation into possible gall bladder inflammation or stones. On another occasion she was suddenly and violently sick, a very rare event for her. Over a period of six to eight weeks the pains migrated to her abdomen but seemed to move around, so that they were difficult to pin-point and to describe to her GP. The swelling due to the ascites became noticeable around six weeks from the start of the initial pains. She became increasingly lethargic and lost her appetite.

In Stage III cases surgery to remove as much tumour as possible is advisable coupled with chemotherapy. Surgery may precede chemotherapy or follow it. In Linda's case she was prescribed a 'sandwich course' of chemotherapy followed by surgery followed by more chemotherapy.

If the cancer has spread beyond the abdomen this is classified as Stage IV ovarian cancer. Around 10% of women with the disease are diagnosed at this stage. Symptoms may be the same as for Stage III cases but with added breathlessness or a cough as the lungs are often involved. Treatment of Stage IV cancer may be by chemotherapy with or without surgery.

It is difficult to define what steps a woman could take to reduce the risk of developing ovarian cancer. Linda gleaned from various reference books that there are five factors which make it less likely. They are having children, breast feeding, taking the contraceptive pill, having a relatively early menopause and having a healthy diet. As she complied with all five she could be excused if she feels somewhat aggrieved that she contracted the disease against the odds.

LINDA'S JOURNAL

HOW THINGS CAN CHANGE

The year started so well. In January 1997 I had my 50th birthday and a party with lots of old friends representing phases of my life dating back to schooldays. The one person missing was our daughter who was taking a year out after graduating to travel around Australia.

A week later we set off for a week's cruise on the Nile – a birthday present from Roy. It was a brilliant experience and prolonged the feeling of celebration. I had reached the age of 50, fit, healthy and active, never seriously ill. How things can change.

I can look back and remember almost exactly when the pains started. But they didn't really seem important at the time. I think it's the same with most people with the odd twinge that doesn't seem to want to go away. "Doctor, I've got this pain." "When did it start?" "Oh, about three weeks ago. Or was it four?" And that's what gets recorded in your medical record. Unless, of course, you can connect the pain with a specific event, a fall, for instance, or slipping and twisting an ankle. Over the years I've had various bits of damage as a result of playing badminton and naturally I've had to stop playing until the thing had mended.

This is different. In early May I become conscious of a vague discomfort in my right shoulder and right rib cage. I assume I have pulled or strained something playing badminton. I know that we are soon going to Brittany with our friends Trevor and Elaine for a week and that the following Monday (normally badminton evening) is a bank holiday and I feel sure that a couple of weeks without playing will solve the problem.

It doesn't.

I even resort to trying pain killers which I don't like doing for any length of time as I feel they mask the problem without really providing a cure. I persist with analgesics/anti-inflammatory pills while we are on holiday and the array of assorted medications that three of us – Elaine, Roy and I – are taking for various aches and pains lined up at mealtimes cause much amusement.

One morning around the middle of the holiday I wake early with a sharper pain than before, just below my ribs. I lie in bed hoping that it will go away. I have become resigned to the fact that I will need to seek expert attention and treatment for my pains but I really hope it can wait until we're back home. I don't want the hassle of sorting out medical treatment in France if I can avoid it. Fortunately the pain subsides and I am able to carry on normally for the rest of the holiday. We spend Friday walking on the beach, climbing on rocks and poking around in rock pools like a group of 50+-year old kids!

By the time we return from France I am becoming a bit fed up. I've had the pains for about three weeks and the break has not made an ounce of difference. The lack of strenuous exercise appears on the other hand to have added inches to my waistline. I had sorted out summer clothes before we left and only tried them on as and when I changed into them during the holiday. Most things now feel noticeably tighter than they did the previous year and, when I can, I surreptitiously leave undone the top buttons on skirts and trousers. My bulging tummy is subtly concealed by blouse or T-shirt.

The two days after our return from France are spent getting the garden sorted out for the summer. I find that bending down is uncomfortable but ignore the problem as there's a lot to be done.

Around 5a.m on Tuesday May 27 I wake with an intense pain below my ribs. This is nothing like the pain of the last few weeks – this I can't ignore and Roy phones the emergency doctor. This is not the sort of thing I make a habit of. I don't think I have needed a home visit from a doctor since I was a child. My details are taken and shortly after the doctor on duty calls back to ask further questions. As I am capable of answering her questions myself it is presumed that I am not actually dying and I am given the choice of going to the A & E department of the local hospital or waiting until my local surgery opens at 8.30. I decide to do the latter and get an appointment almost immediately. My GP thinks I probably have gallstones, which is something we ourselves have thought of as a possibility.

I am sent for the first of many tests. At each stage during the following weeks I am convinced that the next test or examination will provide the answer or some clue to the cause of the problem but for a long time we hit nothing but dead ends. The first test is an ultrasound scan which I am sure will show up some stones. Nothing. I go directly for a chest x-ray and a small shadow shows on my right lung. The procedure has to be repeated as the radiologist thinks I may not have breathed in deeply enough as she took the x-ray. This is because it hurt so much to breath deeply. I try again and the shadow looks smaller but is still there. I am told I have probably have pleurisy but am over the worst. So I go back to my GP for antibiotics which are going to make me better.

Wrong again.

After a couple of weeks the antibiotics are obviously not going to work. By this time I have general abdominal pains which seem to move around. I go to my GP probably two or three times over the next few weeks, but I really feel rather stupid when I have to try to explain that the pain I had last time had gone but I have a pain somewhere else. I mention the fact that I feel I am growing around the middle but he doesn't seem to take this very seriously – I guess this is expected of middle-aged women!

At one stage I have a blood test and, as the nurse is taking my blood sample, she asks why it has to be tested. When I explain my symptoms she suggests that it could be related to a problem with my back. She recommends a chiropractor and I visit him soon after. He examines me, lists all the shortcomings of my spine and sets to work. The experience is quite pleasant until the final hip and neck crunching and even this is not really painful. After all, what middle-aged woman is going to object to having her back massaged by a tall, blond good-looking young man? However, after five or six sessions he admits that he doesn't feel he is really getting to the root of the problem. I promise to keep in touch and let him know when (if ever) someone comes up with a diagnosis.

During the next few weeks things gradually get worse but, because it is gradual, it is only as I look back, I realise now just how ill I felt. During late July my boss, John, goes on holiday so my three day a week job becomes almost full time. It is a real effort to do my ten minute walk to the office, and by the end of a day's work it is even harder to walk back home. When I get home I lie flat on my back for about half an hour until my abdomen starts to feel more comfortable.

I gradually go off my food (this is unheard of!) and it becomes a real effort to eat. Towards the end of July our friends Tim and Tory come to dinner. Tim has a long history of stomach problems and suffers from coeliac disease and has to be careful about what he eats. He is very sympathetic about my odd pains. We have planned a barbecue but the weather is not so good so I grill kebabs indoors. The next day we roast a chicken for lunch, but I am not feeling like eating much so I dish up a small portion. We sit at the table on the patio in the sun but after a few mouthfuls I cannot face any more and tell Roy I am going indoors to lie down. Soon after, I start to vomit. I am most concerned about last night's visitors, especially Tim with his medical history, and phone to ask if they are feeling OK. Fortunately they are. I have not poisoned them!

"I THINK WE NEED SOME HELP"

Eventually my GP says, "I think we need some help." He has run out of ideas. So he refers me to a specialist, a gastro-enterologist, who of course is on holiday so there is another 2 week delay. On July 29 I have my first meeting with Dr Levi who asks me endless questions and then examines me. He immediately comments on the fact that I am very bloated. I have an abdominal x-ray and an appointment is made for a colonoscopy the following Saturday. He warns me that the worst part of the procedure is the emptying of the lower intestines with the aid of "Clean Prep". He is right.

On Friday afternoon I leave work early as I have to start taking the medication at 3 pm. I have 50ml of Senna followed by three sachets of Clean Prep each of which makes a litre of a delicious drink tasting of a mixture of salt and vanilla. I have to drink the three litres in two hours. After about the first half hour the Senna starts to take effect and I spend most of the evening on the loo. Our son calls in during the early evening but I am not good company and have to keep leaving the room!

The colonoscopy is done under 'mild sedation'. Fortunately it knocks me out cold and I am aware of nothing until I come round and am told that I have had not only a colonoscopy but a gastroscopy as well. What is more I apparently had a conversation with the surgeon between the two procedures when he told me what he was going to do. I remember nothing. I also have an ultrasound scan of my abdomen. Surely all this lot must produce an answer. But no. The colonoscopy shows nothing, the gastroscopy shows an inflamed oesophagus (which prevents him taking samples for biopsy) and possibly a hiatus hernia, and the scan reveals fluid in my abdomen. The latter explains the swelling but none of this really pinpoints the main problem.

The next stage is a CT scan which is booked for the following Thursday but I have to go into hospital the day before to have the ascitic fluid drained so that the scan will be easier to interpret. For this I go to the private wing of the local NHS hospital and suffer the embarrassment of being wheeled to the radiography department by a porter dressed in dark trousers, white shirt and striped waistcoat who looks like a waiter in a smart restaurant. I have quite a long wait during which the porter waits with me and we chat. I don't feel terribly comfortable with my own personal man-servant.

Eventually I go into a room with an ultrasound scanner which the radiographer uses so that he can guide the drainage needle into my abdomen. I think this is the most unpleasant procedure I have had to go through. I am warned that I will feel pressure on my abdomen and am likely to yell as the needle pierces the wall. I oblige. Is this what pregnant women have to go through when they have an amniocentesis? If so I'm glad it wasn't available when I had my children back in the dark ages.

The needle is in place and the bag attached. I am returned to the corridor and have another long wait as all the porters from the private wing are busy. Are they really waiters now serving dinner? While lying there on my trolley I start to feel uncomfortable and sneak a look at my bag. It is full. I attract the attention of a nurse and ask if it can be emptied. She disappears and comes back with a jug labelled 'urine only'. I explain that it isn't actually urine and she goes off again. She comes back with the right jug, and empties the bag, commenting "Yuck, it's all warm." This seems a strange attitude for a nurse and I can't help feeling she'd have a far worse problem on her hands if it wasn't warm!

I finally get back to my room where Roy is waiting. Already the bag is filling up again and he goes to find someone to empty it. In total about three litres of fluid are removed. No wonder I've had trouble doing up my clothes.

I spend that night in the hardest bed I have ever encountered. I can't get comfortable on my back or on my side and even try sleeping in the chair. After very little sleep the night is over. The fluid seems to have finished draining out. A nurse offers me breakfast, but, much as I'd like to eat, I have to be honest and tell her that all I am allowed is a drink containing dye to enhance the CT scan. She obviously hasn't been given this message. It's a good job that whatever is going on in my insides I am compos mentis and able to memorise what should be in my medical notes.

I am portered again to the radiography unit and go this time to the CT room. My drainage tube is removed and I have my scan. Totally painless and, I discover later, totally clear. So, no tumour then. What a relief!

Negative tests are all very well but we don't seem to be getting any nearer to the truth. Dr Levi wants to take some more samples for biopsy which means another gastroscopy. Luckily this does not involve the same sort of preparation as a colonoscopy, just a few hours without eating. It is booked for the following Tuesday. I am delighted at the prospect of spending my pearl wedding anniversary in hospital yet again.

On the afternoon of August 12 I go to the Nuffield Hospital for the gastroscopy. Dr Levi takes lots of samples for biopsy. I also meet Mr Desai who is going to perform a laparoscopy the following Saturday. As all the tests so far have produce nothing conclusive he will make a small incision near my navel and do an exploration with a camera. If he this shows nothing he will do a further examination – a laparotomy which involves a larger cut. As this will be done, if necessary, under the same anaesthetic I have to give permission before the operation.

On Wednesday and Thursday I continue working as John is still on holiday in France. I have kept him informed of my medical progress with frequent e-mails and faxes during the past two and a half weeks but this time we know that if a laparotomy is needed I will be in hospital for several days and he will have to cut short his holiday. As I have already caused Roy to call off his planned visit to Tobago, I am really feeling a terrible nuisance.

DARK DAYS AND MORE FRUSTRATION

I arrive at the hospital at 8am on Friday 15 August. My room is very pleasant but incredibly hot as we are currently experiencing a long heat wave. I go for my operation in the early afternoon, still convinced that I will wake up and find that I have only needed a laparoscopy and that this has produced the answer. As it is, I wake up in the recovery room and I have had a laparotomy. I experience waves of incredible pain such as I have certainly not known since I was going through childbirth and possibly not even then. I am also attached to a drip for the first time in my life. (During the next few months I shall become well accustomed to wheeling a drip around like a large pet, taking clothes on and off over the drip and its stand, getting in and out of bed, going to the loo and showering with my trusty friend standing beside me.)

I return to my room and Roy is soon there. A nurse calls him out on the pretext that there is a phone call for him. I am too dozy to realise that this is most unlikely. He comes back and tells me they have found tumours and that I will need chemotherapy. So much for all my negative scans. At that moment I am in such pain that I feel I could quite willingly die and please can it be soon? This feeling does not last long. Mr Desai calls in to give me a bit more detail. He found tumours around the outside of my bowel and in the omentum (which I have never even heard of).

My initial reaction to the news is dulled by the effects of the anaesthetic. In a strange way I feel some relief that at last my illness has a name, even though 'cancer' is the last name I wanted to hear. At least I can start having some treatment, and maybe, one day in a future I can't begin to imagine, I'll feel better.

I have a very bad night as there is a problem with the analgesia. I have many morphine injections, each of which buys about half an hour's sleep then I wake up and wonder how long I can wait until calling a nurse again to ask for more pain-killers. It's a pain which actually makes me shout out – not the way I usually behave. I am allowed no water but have a small sponge which I can dip into water to moisten my lips which are dry. By the time Roy arrives the next morning I have learnt to put my ante-natal lessons from twenty five years ago into practice and find that when I feel a wave of pain coming, sometimes I can divert it by panting. This takes all my concentration and makes me not very exciting company. When the night staff go off duty and the day staff arrive they re-think the situation and I am given a mixture of morphine and pethedine. Relief comes very soon.

I am helped into a chair and get much more comfortable. I spend most of the day dozing. Every time I try to read the newspaper or watch television I just fall asleep. Until I pass wind I am not allowed anything solid to eat. I can have only consommé and jelly. Roy however does justice to the extensive menu on offer. After leaving the hospital on Friday evening he started the job of breaking the news to those closest to us, visiting my mother to tell her personally and phoning our children and John.

That night I ask if I can sleep in the chair as I am more comfortable than I was in bed. This is not allowed so a nurse helps me into bed and I have a much better night. On Sunday I am more awake and can concentrate better on books, newspapers and television. Dr Levi pays a visit with his young son. He is so kind and sympathetic. It is a hot sunny day and Roy and I go for our first walk in the grounds. I am still restricted to consommé and jelly (and one portion of fruit sorbet!) for obvious reasons. The wind is rumbling around but doesn't emerge. (No, I am not talking about the weather.)

I think my attitude becomes more positive and hope that the chemotherapy will start very soon. In retrospect, I am glad that I didn't know at that stage how long a delay there would be.

Early on Monday morning I pass wind and can wait only until 7.15 to phone Roy to tell him the news. When Mr Desai calls in, fortunately quite early, I tell him of my success and he tells me to order breakfast and that I can go home in the afternoon. Who would believe that so much could depend on a single fart?

During the morning I have a visit from Dr Parry-Williams, the senior GP at our local practice who originally suggested that I may have gallstones. Roy spoke to him the day before when he was visiting another patient and told him the news. He was shocked to find out the diagnosis but is pleased that I have a positive attitude.

When Roy comes we go for another walk in the grounds, have lunch and then prepare for going home. The staff have all been so kind and supportive and I expect to see them again when I return to the Nuffield for chemotherapy.

It's good to get back home. The weather is still very hot so I sit in the garden. It's difficult to find clothes to wear as the laparotomy cut was made in such a position that anything touching my waist rubs it.

Friends and neighbours keep phoning or visiting with offers of help and words of encouragement. Over the next few weeks get well cards and letters arrive as more people hear the news.

The day after I come home, Roy is out shopping and there is a ring at the door. Dr Parry-Williams is there clutching a parcel. He explains that he didn't want to bring flowers but rather, something more personal, something he had caught himself. The parcel contains a large frozen trout which he had caught on his latest fishing holiday. I am very touched by his kind thought.

We arrange for Edward and Nicola to come for a barbecue that evening. We are also expecting Mr L to come and discuss our wills with us as we have decided to update them. The appointment had been made long before we were aware that events would make his visit so appropriate.

During the afternoon there is a call from Mr Desai who wants us to go to see him at the Nuffield that evening. I explain that we have plans for the evening but he is most insistent that he should see us quickly. I am convinced that such urgency must mean more bad news. We arrange a time so that we can talk briefly to Mr L and then leave Edward in charge of cooking while we go to the hospital. He is also left to explain our apparent rudeness to Mr L.

It turns out that the news is good. Although the first tumour Mr Desai saw was around the bowel he was never convinced that it had originated there. Further examinations suggest that the site of origin is one or both of my ovaries. The extent of the spread of the tumours sounds horrendous but he assures me that the prognosis is better than if it had started in the bowel as ovarian cancer responds well to chemotherapy. A blood test for a marker known as CA125 will confirm the site of origin. He will refer me to Dr Ashford, an oncologist.

Again there is more delay as Dr Ashford is on holiday and we can't get an appointment for two weeks. We are assured that a delay of this length is of no consequence but I am getting desperate to start the treatment. At some point during this wait I have a visit from Eileen who lives nearby. She has heard about me via another neighbour who thought I might like to talk to her. Eileen was treated for acute leukaemia about 5 years ago and now looks a picture of health. In many ways her situation was far worse than mine as she had very young children and had to be kept in isolation for months while she had chemotherapy. One thing in particular that she says remains with me. She says that chemo doesn't have to be as bad as most reports suggest. One hears so much about the awful side effects that it's nice to hear of someone who's been through it and not found it too unbearable.

Someone else I contact during these early stages is the chiropractor I consulted in June/July. He had asked me to keep in touch as he was interested in finding out the diagnosis. He suggests I contact Ms D for counselling and advice. I phone her for an appointment which is made for about 3 weeks ahead as she is about to go on holiday. In the meantime, we have quite a long chat on the phone. Two pieces of advice stick in my mind. The first is that she advises me to 'get into therapy'. I'm not too sure what this means but it doesn't sound like my sort of thing. I don't feel I'm a therapy sort of person. Even at this early stage I don't feel the need for professional psychological help – I have a disease and it will be treated. Whether the treatment will be successful or not I will not know for a long time, but I don't think I have a problem facing it.

Her other piece of advice is that I should read a particular book. It has to be ordered but as soon as I get it I start to read hoping that there will be some practical advice. It is written by a woman who had malignant melanoma and orthodox treatment provided no long-term answer. She chose to go for the Gerson therapy which involves drinking huge amounts of freshly-prepared organic fruit and vegetable juices together with injections of liquidised raw calves liver and coffee enemas! Now I have no doubt that the therapy worked for this person – she is alive and maybe would not have been without the therapy. However, I find the book one of the most depressing things I have ever read. The therapy takes over the patient's whole life as the preparation involved is so time-consuming, and I really feel that I do not want this disease to dominate my life completely. Just knowing I have the disease is dominating enough and I hope to be able to fit in a reasonably normal life around the treatment.

The book does make me wonder if large amounts of fresh juice might be helpful so we go out and buy a juicer along with fruits and vegetables (as many organic as we can find) and start experimenting. The juice that pours from the machine is frothy and sludgy and separates very quickly into a clear layer and a sludge layer. Apart from the most common varieties such as orange, most taste fairly nasty. Preparing the juice and cleaning the machine takes long enough and the thought of doing the whole Gerson thing (sixteen batches of juice a day) would be very daunting. The novelty soon wears off and I return to my normal diet which I think is reasonably healthy.

I never do make it to see Ms D as the appointment coincides with a later hospital appointment. Perhaps I will one day regret this but for now I decide to follow the conventional route.

We decide early on that we will be completely open about the situation and tell people what is wrong with me. We realise that it is going to be a major factor in our lives, it will affect our interaction with friends and it seems easier to be honest than try to make excuses for refusing invitations etc. We decide that we should tell close friends fairly quickly rather than take the risk that they will hear via other sources. We do discover that news travels very quickly. I find it very difficult to tell friends, to say "I have cancer", although once they know, I am willing to talk about it (I worry about become a real bore on the subject!). Roy does a brilliant PR job and breaks the news to lots of people. Initial reactions vary widely from those who have great faith in modern medicine and are sure that I'll be fine to those who seem far more devastated than I was when I first heard. Some people want to visit immediately while others seem reluctant, not knowing how I'll be and afraid that I will be lying around looking horribly ill. Generally visitors are surprised to find that I don't look ill at all.

At my next consultation with Mr Desai I ask questions about the tumour. I want to find out as much as possible about this alien inside me. Unfortunately he has no idea how long it has been there. Regarding its appearance he explains that, whereas the omentum is normally a soft fatty structure, mine has converted completely to a hard cancerous mass. I still can't imagine what it looks like. Only Mr Desai and his team have actually seen it. He does tell us also that the blood tests have shown a raised CA125 level which confirms the idea that it probably originated in my ovaries.

I go back to work a week after the laparotomy, trying to keep busy and take my mind off this illness which has been occupying our minds so much since May and has become even more so since the diagnosis. On the Friday I come home and have a cup of tea while watching Neighbours. Roy is behaving a bit oddly and eventually says, "Those prawns you've got for dinner won't feed five people you know." So what? There are only two of us. He explains that Helen is due at Heathrow at any time and he has been looking a Ceefax on the other television for information on her flight. I have known for some time that Helen intends to cut short her Australian trip and come home slightly earlier than planned, but I have asked Roy not to tell me exactly when and I certainly didn't expect it to be for another week or two. The plan is that we go to Heathrow to pick her up, Edward and Nicola will come round to put up 'Welcome Home' banners and balloons and we will all have an Indian take-away.

Ceefax tells us absolutely nothing about Helen's flight but, after several phone calls Roy discovers that it has landed so we set off. When we reach the terminal, Helen is just coming through the Arrivals lounge. She looks tired, slightly scruffy and her hair looks greasy, but then she has been travelling for many hours and to me she looks just great. She and I sit in the back of the car on the way home and hold hands. Tired or not she talks non-stop – some things never change!

Ed and Nicola have done their bit and after lots of chatting we order the take-away. It doesn't arrive when it should have done and there are many calls to the restaurant, each more irate than the last before it arrives. Roy and Ed get extremely angry but for me nothing is going to spoil Helen's return. Having a life-threatening illness does help you sort out what is really important.

Finally the day (or rather, evening) arrives for seeing Dr Ashford. Let's hope treatment will follow quickly. We set off for our appointment and end up debating in the car where we are seeing him. I have assumed we have to go to the Nuffield Hospital while Roy thinks it is at South Lodge consulting rooms. We don't have time to go back home to phone to check so we stop at South Lodge as that is the first of the two that we reach. I am relieved that we are in the right place as we don't have much time before our appointment. In the event, it would not have mattered too much if we had been late. The waiting room is full and all the patients are waiting to see Dr Ashford. Most have seen him many times before and the situation always seems to be the same. There is a lot of banter about how long people have had to wait in the past – the winner left around 10.45pm after a 7pm appointment. We realise we have come without our BUPA form and, as there seems to be plenty of time, Roy goes home to collect it, and as we had decided to have dinner after our consultation, he also brings back bananas to stave off the hunger. The receptionist provides coffee, there are plenty of magazines to read and people to talk to, so under different circumstances it would had the potential for being quite a jolly evening. I think I had better get used to the idea of such evenings as there could be many more of them. Perhaps another evening we could take the example of some patients who went to the local pub while waiting.

I finally get to see Dr Ashford. He examines me, checks my notes which by now include my CA125 reading, and agrees that my tumours are almost certainly ovarian in origin. The snag is that Dr Ashford only treats breast cancer and is unwilling to take me on. I have a choice of 2 ovarian cancer specialists, one based at Mount Vernon Hospital and one at the Princess Margaret in Windsor. The latter is more convenient so I take the details of Dr Thomas.

While I am at work the next day, Roy phones Dr Thomas's secretary to make an appointment. Dr Thomas is due to go to a conference in Hamburg and the only consultation session before that is fully booked. Roy explains the situation and how concerned we are at all the delays. We get an appointment for the following Tuesday, September 9.

PROGRESS AT LAST

Dr Thomas is young, reassuring and easy to talk to. She soon discovers that Roy and I have a scientific background and fills us in with lots of detail about the disease and its treatment. I will be treated with Taxol, a relatively new drug and Carboplatin, a drug which has been used for much longer. The chemistry of Taxol is related to derivatives of the yew tree. Taxol seems to improve the prognosis for the patients who receive it, I will have three treatments at three week intervals, then a hysterectomy and three more chemo sessions. Before I can start chemo I have to go to the Hammersmith Hospital for a kidney function test. This measures how fast things travel through my system and will be used to determine the dosage of the chemo drugs needed.

Dr Thomas asks if we would like to meet the sister who will be administering the treatment, so we meet Lorraine. She comes with us to the imaging department where I have to have a chest X-ray, and we spend quite a time chatting. She explains more about the procedures involved and possible side effects. The whole subject is so interesting. I only wish I was not studying it from my current point of view. The most likely problems are aches and pains, tingling and numbness in hands and feet, tiredness and various other minor problems but hopefully not nausea or sickness as I will receive other drugs to counteract these. Lorraine is very kind and reassuring. I feel safe in her hands. If only we could just get on with it.

My kidney function test is arranged for two days later, around 11am. We drive up to the Hammersmith Hospital which is actually in Acton, and park in Wormwood Scrubs car park. We go first to the cancer unit but should be in the radiography department. Having found the right place I am placed in a scanner and have a radioactive tracer injected into my arm. This takes several attempts as the needle doesn't want to stay in place. I then have to lie very still for twenty minutes while the scan is done. The surface I lie on is very hard. I am then told we can do what we want for two hours, then I must return to the cancer department for half-hourly blood tests. No-one can recommend anywhere to eat so we leave the hospital and head for what looks like a busy road. We find just one pub in the area which seems to serve a wide range of food. We sit outside in a small courtyard. It's pretty grotty but there's really no choice and the food is edible.

We walk back to the hospital, wasting a bit of time by trying an alternative route but are sure we have plenty of time. However, when we get to the hospital grounds we cannot find the way to the cancer unit. We know where it is but there just doesn't seem to be a way through. Eventually we get there and register at the desk. I wait. No-one calls me and it is well past two hours since the scan. I go back to the desk and am sent into the chemotherapy unit. Finally someone takes my blood and I'm sent back to the waiting room and told to come back in half an hour. This happens three more times then my cannula is removed and I am free to go. While I am pleased to know that when I have my chemo I will be in a room on my own, it is quite encouraging to see the Hammersmith unit. People are sitting around in armchairs, reading, chatting, listening to Walkmans, even sleeping. The only unusual thing was that they all have drips attached to their arms or to Hickman lines. They are having chemo but it seems to be no big deal. This is very comforting.

There is now nothing we can do to speed things up so we decide to go away for the weekend as it is Roy's birthday. On Saturday 13 September we drive to Canterbury where we have booked one night in the County Hotel. Why Canterbury? Because Roy has never been there and I have not been for more years than I like to admit to. After 'doing' the cathedral, having lunch and generally wandering around we end up in the shopping area and start to browse in book shops. I go straight to the medical department and find there is little written about ovarian cancer. Each general book has a small section which I read and gradually I piece together my situation. I am in the third stage of the disease (which I already knew) and, statistically, the prospects of living for another five years are not good. On the other hand, statistically I shouldn't have the disease anyway. I find there are five factors which make it less likely that a woman develops ovarian cancer – having children, breast feeding, having taken the contraceptive pill, having a relatively early menopause and having a healthy diet. I have done all of these things so decide not to let statistics rule my life. Also, the statistics relating to patients who have had Taxol were not available when these books were written as the drug is too new, so I can only hope that in my case Taxol will live up to its 'miracle drug' reputation.

We eventually reach September 24 – the day of the first chemo. The previous night at 11pm and again at 5am I have to take ten tablets – with food! These are the first of a cocktail of drugs which supplement the main chemo drugs and minimise the side-effects. I am very nervous. Whatever people tell you to reassure you, nothing can really prepare one for something so unknown.

I arrive at the Princess Margaret Hospital in Windsor at 10 am and am taken to a room on the first floor. I am armed with books and newspaper as I expect a very long boring day. There is already a drip stand in the room and a tray with syringes and phials and bags containing drugs. Lorraine arrives and tries to insert a cannula. For some reason it won't stay put at the first two attempts. She calls the RMO who tries a vein in the other arm and succeeds immediately. The first job is to take a blood sample for testing to make sure I am up to the treatment. Everything's fine so my vein is flushed with saline solution then Lorraine injects four different drugs to counteract nausea, allergic reactions, etc. She then changes the 'giving set' – the system of tubes and valves through which the drugs are administered – as Taxol needs a special set. It will eat through the normal plastic tubes so a special material has to be used – hopefully it will eat through the unwanted bits in my abdomen without too much damage to the healthy areas. Taxol is very thick so drips in slowly – it takes about three hours.

Roy stays with me and people pop in and out of the room and we chat a lot. Sabine, a Belgian nurse, is shadowing Lorraine and we reminisce about our time in Belgium. Lorraine explains more about what the next few months will involve. Each chemo session will be on a Wednesday. By the first weekend I am likely to feel achy, tired, rather 'fluey'. About a week after the chemo my immune system will start to suffer and for about a week I will have to be careful about picking up infections. This means avoiding as far as possible crowded busy places. For the final week between chemo sessions I should be feeling fine.

We have coffee, then lunch. Around 2pm the drip is changed and the carboplatin is administered over about one more hour. The day turns out to be such a chatty social occasion that the newspaper is barely opened, our books are unread and the day flies by. I leave the hospital around 3.30pm armed with tablets to take over the next three days and another twenty to take before the second session. I also have fact sheets on taxol and carboplatin explaining the side-effects I can expect. These tend to be cumulative and so are likely to be more pronounced as the treatment progresses.

That night I do not sleep very well but do not immediately associate it with the treatment. The next day I have stabbing pains in my abdomen, my face is flushed and I have pains in my chest when I walk. A few days after the treatment I start to feel hungry. I don't mean 'a bit peckish', I mean ravenously, obsessively hungry. I sit at my desk and by 10am I am thinking about lunch whereas normally at work I am often so engrossed that I may not have lunch until 1.30, even 2 o'clock. As soon as I have had lunch I start to think about dinner! Fortunately this does not last many days and I am very relieved when, during my second chemo session, Lorraine says I may find that I tend to put on weight during the treatment as a result of one of the drugs which is a steroid.

At least I know there is a reason for my hunger and that it will soon go away. My hearing is also affected – sounds seem to echo inside my head when I talk and I don't hear other people very clearly. I develop a dark smudge on my left wrist where my metal watch strap is and have to dig out an old watch with a plastic strap. If the sweat on my wrist contains enough chemicals to eat my watch what on earth is going on in my insides?

These effects wear off in a few days and have little impact on my normal life. In fact, we have a very active week socially with visits to and from friends. I continue to work which greatly helps to take my mind off my illness – if I don't have enough to keep my mind busy it is all too easy to start imagining symptoms.

I go to the hospital on the Wednesdays between chemos for a blood test but otherwise carry on life as normal (well, almost).

Lorraine has given me details of a lady in Maidenhead who supplies wigs. Roy persuades me that I should do something about getting one as soon as possible rather than waiting until there are signs that my hair is falling out. We make an appointment for September 29 and I go along and try a whole range of colours and styles. Being a person who likes to merge into the background I resist the idea of blond dreadlocks and choose one as close to my own hair as possible. It is ordered and arrives within a few days so I make another appointment to collect it and have it trimmed. It feels hot and itchy. Will I really ever get used to wearing it? I am grateful that I am having my treatment during the colder weather.

Two weeks after the first chemo a clump of pubic hair falls out. I know that I will lose virtually all my hair but have hoped that it would happen later rather than sooner. At least it's not started anywhere noticeable. But, the next day, it starts to fall out of my head. We have planned a weekend away – a couple of days in the New Forest before the next session. We have a lovely weekend, we walk a lot and I am feeling fine except for a slight obsession about leaving clumps of hair everywhere. On the way home on the Sunday we call in on Kim, a friend from Brussels who is now back in Fareham. I am rather embarrassed about the hair problem but she assures me that it isn't noticeable.

Wednesday, October 15 is the second chemo day and follows the same pattern as the first. The side-effects are similar to the first time. On October 17 we visit our friends Trevor and Elaine in Lichfield. I feel that my hair by now is conspicuously thin but I am persuaded to go out to lunch without the wig. I know it won't be possible for much longer. Before we leave Trevor and Elaine the wig has its first public viewing. No-one falls about laughing but are they just being polite? I keep it on while we drive to pick up Roy's father who is coming to stay for the weekend. He doesn't notice straight away and is rather confused as Roy has warned him that I am losing my hair. I begin to accept that it does look quite natural.

The hair carries on falling out faster and faster. I can remove large clumps and when I wash it the plug hole gets blocked. I've had enough of this so on October 23 I ask Roy to use his beard trimmer to shave it to the length of a very short crew-cut. This feels more comfortable and avoids the problem of leaving hairs everywhere.

As the months go on the wig becomes a sort of family pet and the butt of constant jokes. We have photos of all the family wearing it as it gets passed around at family gatherings. We have jokes like "If *you* want to wear it *you* feed it/take it for a walk".

"THERE IS NO CURE"

The next stage in the treatment is to arrange to have surgery. I go to the Hammersmith Hospital for my first meeting with Mr McIndoe on October 24. I am expecting that the main point of this meeting is to arrange a date for the hysterectomy. However it seems it is not so clear-cut. He makes no promise that surgery will improve my prognosis. In fact he actually says "There is no cure." He warns me that it is a major operation and may not solve any problems. It is up to us to decide whether or not to go ahead. I instinctively feel that removing the sites where the cancer started has to be a good thing. Whether this is true or not I don't really know. Mr McIndoe does sway us to a certain extent by saying that if it were his wife, he would advise her to have the operation. The operation is planned for late November at the Wellington Hospital. It will be roughly three weeks after the third chemo session on the basis that if I'm fit enough for more chemo I'm fit enough for the operation.

The next five weeks follow a similar routine to the previous few weeks. I am able to work almost my full number of days, just having a couple of days off when I really do feel too tired. Our treat before the third chemo is a weekend away staying with friends near the Forest of Dean. We have a brilliant time. I feel fine and we are able to do plenty of walking and exploring in an area we have never visited before. The wig again meets with approval.

Wednesday Nov 5. I have my third chemo session and at the end of the afternoon Lorraine tells me about Avril who is having her treatment in a different order from mine. She had her hysterectomy about three weeks ago and today is having her first chemo. She suggests that it could be useful for both of us if we meet for a chat so I go along to her room. She tells me about her experiences in the Wellington hospital and I talk about the side effects I have had from the chemo. When, some weeks later, I am filling in a questionnaire about the hospital – questions like 'How much information were you given before your stay in hospital', I realise just how useful this conversation with Avril was, giving me far more practical information than I could have got from the more formal facts dished out by the hospital authorities.

We decide not to go away again before the operation. There is quite a lot to get ready before I go to hospital as I expect to be away for about ten days and I need to do as much as possible in preparation for Christmas. I know I won't be able to do much when I come home. We do however go to Cheltenham for a day and explore the town and do some shopping.

On Tuesday November 26, Roy and I meet up with an old colleague of his for lunch. This is the first time I have met Roger although he has been a bad influence on Roy for many years. I have always known that 'lunch with Roger' means 'I'll be back fairly late in the evening, very much worse for wear.' Roy has assured me that I will like him and I do. He is charming and very easy to get on with. I leave the two of them in the restaurant after lunch as I have planned to visit my mother. I arrive at Garrick house, the sheltered accommodation where she lives and am summoned by a member of staff who tells me that Mum has been taken to Wexham Park Hospital. She has suffered for many years with arthritis and this morning was particularly immobile. Her GP has said that she should go to hospital for observation and for some help with her mobility. We phone the hospital and discover she is still waiting in A&E. I decide to go home and keep contacting the hospital so that I can visit her as soon as she is placed in a ward.

I phone the hospital numerous times and am told 'she has been seen but is waiting for an X-ray', 'she is waiting to see somebody else', etc., etc. until at 7.30 I am told that she will be in ward 8A within an hour. I allow plenty of time and leave home at 9pm. At ward 8A I am told that they are expecting her some time but don't know when. I go to the A&E department and find her lying on a trolley where she has been since around 3pm. She has been seen by several different members of the hospital staff and has had an X-ray. She has been told she may have had a minor stroke. She has been offered nothing to eat or drink. Now I wish I had come to the hospital sooner but my decision seemed to be the right one at the time. By 10.30 there has been a little progress and it seems that she will soon be transferred to the ward. By this time I am not feeling too brilliant and Mum insists that I should go home.

Eventually, she spent a week in hospital and improved because she was given some different tablets. Apart from this, all she gained was a cough and bed sores. (The latter are still being treated months later.) I contrast this with the treatment I have been receiving and am so glad we have continued to pay for health insurance since Roy stopped working.

On Wednesday November 26, my last working day for who knows how long, John and I go across the road to the Stag for lunch. He gives me a get well card and a small gift-wrapped box to be opened on Saturday when I need cheering up. After work I visit Mum in hospital and then go home to get my own things ready for the next day.

On Thursday, November 27 Roy and I go by train to St John's Wood and then walk to the Wellington Hospital. It is the usual pre-operation sort of day – details of what is going to happen, visits from the surgeon and anaesthetist, etc. During the afternoon the first of many bouquets arrives – these are from Kim and Heather. Kim had cancer recently and was one of the first people I discussed my condition with back in August. Now, he looks a picture of health and like so many other friends, is very encouraging and supportive.

I am to be given the dreaded Clean Prep again but am relieved to find that I only have to have one litre around 4pm and another litre tomorrow morning. This is a doddle compared with the three litres I had to drink on the previous occasion. After the first litre I am limited to liquids only until the next morning when the 'Nil by Mouth' sign goes up on the door. Roy leaves in the early evening and I know the next day will be very difficult for him. We have decided that there is no point in him trekking all the way to the hospital on the day of the operation so he just has to try to keep busy at home.

Friday November 28 is a long day as the operation is scheduled for 4pm. I read the newspaper, watch daytime TV, do my tapestry and chat with a succession of nurses. In the early afternoon I change into the very becoming theatre gown and thigh length tight white stockings. I remember the journey to the operating theatre and the chat as I am wired up to monitors and given an injection. Then nothing until I wake up in the recovery room. The nurse tells me I am to be taken back to my room very soon and I want to say 'No. That's not right. I'm supposed to spend tonight in Intensive Care. It's all booked.' Unfortunately, I'm not awake enough to say anything, so I start to wonder what's happened. Has Mr McIndoe opened me up and decided that there's nothing he can do?

Back in my room I find that I have a PCA (patient controlled analgesia) device attached to my left hand, a drip in the right and a catheter. The PCA is a wonderful machine which allows me to administer a shot of morphine whenever I need it (within reason – I can't overdose!). The drip will make sure I don't die of starvation while I am unable to eat. The catheter is very uncomfort but does provide protection to organs which have taken quite a battering by eliminating the pressure produced by having a full bladder.

I am extremely dozy for the rest of the day (some would say this is normal) but at around 10pm I ask the nurse to pass me the phone and I call home. I probably don't make much sense but I feel the family might like to hear from me. Before settling down for the night I have an anti-coagulant injection directly into my stomach. I remember these from my previous stay in hospital when I had the laparotomy – they hurt.

I get through the night with the help of my PCA until around 6am I have a repeat of the intense pains I had after the first laparotomy. I call the nurse and there is some delay while a doctor is contacted to change my prescription. A shot of Omnipon relieves the pain. At 11am two nurses decide that I can get out of bed and help me into the chair. They have been too ambitious and it is too soon – I vomit, and they put me back to bed. Around this time, Roy arrives and stays for the whole day. I am not good company as I sleep most of the time, but he doesn't mind as there is rugby on television!

"WE WERE VERY PLEASED"

I am much reassured on the following morning when the anaesthetist comes to my room to report on the operation. It turns out that I have responded so well to chemotherapy that Mr McIndoe believes he has been able to remove all the tumours which have shrunk significantly and become detached from the organs. It has not been necessary to put in any drains and I don't need intensive care.

More flowers arrive – deep purple tulips from Roy and an arrangement from his colleagues at Groundwork, some of whom I have met just once. I am very touched by their concern. I also open my present from John – a pair of lovely silver earrings. The day passes in a haze as I drift in and out of sleep. I drink only water until dinner time when I have a few sips of clear soup. At bedtime I have the dreaded anti-coagulant injection but this evening's duty nurse takes pity on me and, as my abdomen has taken quite a battering, she injects it into my arm. Still painful but not so bad.

On Sunday morning I feel much better. I eat a few corn flakes and drink half a cup of coffee. I am helped into the chair around 9am. Roy arrives with Edward and Helen who bring more flowers. The boys go off to the pub for lunch while Helen stays with me and eats most of my lunch after I have eaten the minute amount that I can manage. During the afternoon someone comes to clean my room and this seems a good time to venture out from the four walls. I need the family's help with moving around with all my attachments. I must be a strange spectacle sitting by the nurses' station with drip, PCA, catheter and no hair but I don't care. This is progress. Roy and the 'children' leave in the early evening for the drive back home.

That night I encounter the one nurse with whom I do have a slight problem. All the other staff have been brilliant – so kind and caring and the great thing about the private sector is that they have time for a chat and to explain things. But when this particular nurse (I only ever saw her this one evening) helps me to get back into bed it is like a scene from 'Fawlty Towers' as she battles with the drip etc. Somehow I do end up in bed in one piece. I shall be glad to lose all these contraptions although I am really very grateful for them. The cannulas are making my hands sore and the catheter is most uncomfortable.

After a small breakfast on Monday I am deemed to be eating again so the drip can be removed as is the PCA as any pain can now be controlled by tablets. I am helped to shower and the dressing is removed revealing a ladder of staples about 9inches long, vertically up my abdomen. I put on a clean nightie, my new earrings, make-up and my wig so that I'm starting to look almost human. Two more lots of flowers arrive from Roy's Dad and from a company which I deal with a lot at work. Most of the people at this company I have never met – I just speak to them on the phone, but word has reached them about my condition and again I'm amazed to find how caring people are. I also receive loads of cards. It's just as well I have a large room as every surface is becoming occupied by flowers and cards. Flower maintenance becomes a daily job as I go round with a glass of water (nothing heavy must be lifted) to top up the vases and arrangements and I suspect that some of the nurses spend extra time with me because my room looks and smells so wonderful!

Mr McIndoe visits in the evening and confirms what the anaesthetist said – that the tumour had shrunk a great deal and was removable. I can go home on Friday if I feel up to it. This is good news as I had expected to stay until early next week.

On Tuesday I resume an independent existence when the catheter is removed. This is simpler than expected and I hardly felt anything. Resuming normal bladder use presents no problem. Roy calls in briefly and then leaves for a meeting, but not before Helen arrives unexpectedly. I knew she had a day off work but I thought she had other plans.

On Wednesday, Roy doesn't visit – he needs a break from trekking up to London every day. I pass the time doing my tapestry, reading and watching TV – the sort of things one can't spend all day doing at home without feeling guilty. And there is the flower maintenance to be done and the occasional stroll around the hospital corridors. During the afternoon, Sister Mary asks if I have 'done the stairs' yet. I haven't and can see the need to practice before coming home where I will have to go up and down stairs. We go down two flights stopping between flights to look out of the windows. She points out landmarks although it is getting rather dark. This is the easy bit. We then have to climb back up the two flights and by the time I get back to my room I am quite puffed out. I do hate feeling so feeble.

Helen and Jamie visit in the evening. They had said they might come but weren't sure. It was really nice to see them even though within minutes of arriving Jamie had summoned a nurse by pressing a switch in the bathroom!

On Thursday morning I wake up to find that it has been snowing. One of the New Zealand nurses is excited at the prospect that there could be a white Christmas. I am glad to have a good excuse for not budging from the warmth of my room. Roy spends most of the day with me and takes me on a second stair walk. This is less tiring than the day before. I am starting to feel a bit nervous about coming home although I am looking forward to it. I have been pampered and cosseted for the past week and have had no responsibility for anything but me and my flowers. The nurses warn me to expect to feel extremely tired when I get home as a result of doing no more than just pottering about more than I have been.

Friday is going home day. I am given some staple removers to take to our local surgery when I go on Tuesday to have my stitches out. Roy would love to do the job himself but I think I'll feel safer in the hands of our nurse. By the time Roy arrives to collect me I have put all my things together ready for packing, taken down my cards and put my bouquets (more have been delivered by this time) into carrier bags. It looks as if he will need several trips down to the car to load everything but a porter comes with a trolley to help out.

Being back in the outside world again is strange. I feel I have been in my cocoon for much more than a week. When I am back home I must remember not to do anything strenuous. I know it won't be easy as so many actions we all do are spontaneous, like picking up things from the floor or reaching for something on a high shelf. All these are forbidden for a couple of weeks followed by a very gradual process of getting back to normal. I will have to keep asking for help which doesn't come naturally. Roy has been developing his culinary skills over the last few months but still likes some guidance. A major test will come in a few weeks when he will have to cook the Christmas dinner.

At first it is quite easy to sit around giving out instructions – I don't feel up to doing much else. I sort out the flowers which just about fitted into the boot of the car but have to ask Roy to lift the vases.

Some weeks ago our friends Andrew and Margaret invited us for dinner on Saturday December 6. Originally we expected that I would still be in hospital, so Roy decided to go alone. In the event I am at home. They only live 3 doors away and it would be nice to go out. But I do wonder if it would be really stupid to go out socialising the day after my return home. I decide to go. First I have to find something reasonably smart to wear. Clothes are a real problem as most do sit right on the waist and rub the scar. I find a skirt with an elastic waistband which is long enough to hitch up above the sensitive area. It is a most enjoyable evening but by 1030 I am very tired so come home leaving Roy behind.

On Monday I find that I am bleeding slightly and am worried that I have been too ambitious. I take it very easy.

On Tuesday I have an appointment with the nurse at the local surgery to have my staples removed. It's not far away – normally only a few minutes' walk so we don't take the car.

However it takes longer than normal. Most of the staples come out cleanly and easily but a few are more stubborn and really pull. Kathy, the nurse suggests taking out alternate staples today and the rest tomorrow, but eventually decides that the scar is healing well and she can safely remove them all. I am relieved to get it over and done with and not to have to come back again, especially as tomorrow, just twelve days after the operation, I start chemo again. Just in case I should start to feel better after the operation, they're going to zap me with more chemicals. It seems as if they're determined to keep me down somehow!

I discuss the recent bleeding and she and the GP on duty reassure me that it is quite normal after such an operation. There is no need to worry unless it lasts for several weeks and/or is very bright red.

I spend quite a time at the surgery updating Kathy on all that has happened since she suggested that my symptoms could all relate to a back problem and while we chat Roy goes home to fetch the car as I don't feel I can cope with that long walk home.

BACK TO THE OLD ROUTINE

The day of chemo 4 follows the now familiar pattern. However, the effects afterwards are rather more drastic than on previous occasions. My joints ache more and the tiredness lasts for about a week. Still, this is hardly surprising after the punishment my body's been taking recently. For the first few days after leaving the Wellington I have not felt as tired as I expected to, but this 4th session of chemo really hits me.

The first weekend after this, on Sunday December 14, we have been invited to Rod and Val's for pre-Christmas lunch-time drinks. I decide to go – it would be nice to see them. We only stay for about an hour as I find that standing, even for a short time, is uncomfortable and makes me feel dizzy.

Later in the day I find that the bleeding which had subsided has started again. Perhaps I stood up for too long. The next day I consult Dr Dalton who reassures me that it is not unusual after such an operation.

Flowers still keep arriving from friends who have assumed that I would have lots while in hospital and thought it would be better to wait until I am back home. There are calls most days from people asking how I am and again Roy resumes his PR job where possible, filling in the details, so that I don't have to keep repeating the whole story, as I find talking on the phone quite tiring. Friends call in for cups of tea but are all very understanding and considerate. They don't stay long – they just want to see how I am. I continue to be amazed and grateful that so many people care so much.

The first time I walk all the way to the village I am convinced that someone has moved it while I've been away – it seems so much further than normal! I am so pleased that I work in an office in the middle of the village – it means there is always somewhere to stop for a break before setting off home again.

By the time Christmas arrives I am feeling reasonably fit and have to keep reminding myself that I have to take things easy. Everyone rallies round to help with all the extra jobs which have to be done at this time of year, in particular, Roy cooks the Christmas dinner with a bit of supervision and it's a great success.

Chemo 5 is scheduled for New Year's Eve. As I usually feel quite lively for the first day or two after treatment I don't expect this to be a problem. While I am at the hospital Dr Thomas comes in and talks about a drug trial she would like me to be involved in. She doesn't go into much detail – if I am interested she will refer me to a colleague. I think I'll go for it – there seems nothing to lose. She also tells me that my hair is likely to start growing again which seems so strange – why should it start after the fifth session?

We go to Eddy and Janet's for dinner, keeping up a long-standing tradition of celebrating the New Year with them and Andrew and Margaret. We have arranged to stay the night just in case I do feel tired and need to go to bed early. In the event, I am probably the one who has least trouble staying awake into the early hours of January 1, thanks to my 3-weekly dose of steroids. I certainly hope that 1998 is an improvement on '97.

January 14 is the day of my post-operative check-up with Mr McIndoe. We go up to Harley Street having had the choice of seeing him there or at the Hammersmith Hospital, or the Wellington. I feel I might as well add another to my list of places I've been treated or examined at so we decide on a day out in London. I'm feeling fine except for the odd twinge but even so the walk from the station to the consulting rooms seems quite a distance. Perhaps I'm not as fit as I like to think I am. After my examination, Mr McIndoe's attitude is quite different from when I first met him – he is so much more positive. With my extremely good response to the chemo and the unexpected simplicity of the operation things are looking a lot better than they were in October. He confirms that I can really start to get back to a normal life. This includes resuming our sex life the absence of which has, not surprisingly, bothered Roy more than me over the last 6 weeks.

After the consultation we go for lunch and celebrate with a bottle of wine and then we wander round the shops. I'm a bit sore where Mr McIndoe has had to apply silver nitrate to an area where I had not healed completely, but I don't want to concentrate too much on these minor irritations – I am after all still alive.

I am very nervous about our first post-op sexual activity but find that a gentle session doesn't cause any problems.

Two days later I have another ultra-sound scan, just because it is normal to have one at this stage. I don't have a great deal of faith in these scans as all the early ones I had showed nothing and, as expected, this one is also clear.

My final chemo session is on January 21, the day before my 51st birthday. I haven't specially enjoyed being 50 – it hasn't been at all as it was supposed to be. It is only in the middle of the night as I'm sitting in bed reading, unable to sleep as usual after chemo that it suddenly hits me that the chemo is finally over, for now at least. I think back to last September when we were trying to work out when the chemo would come to an end and now we've made it. Nothing about the future is certain – it never can be – but it's looking a more hopeful than it did 4 months ago.

STARDOM AND TRIALS

The effects of the final chemo are not as bad as the previous two. I gradually become stronger. We have some beautiful warm days during February and on one of these we go for the longest walk I've done for ages – we walk about 5 miles in the Pangbourne area. It is quite windy and I suddenly realise that I have lost even the fine hairs on my face. I feel specks of dust and grit hitting my face and stinging where normally those tiny hairs would offer protection. The general hair situation is confusing. Some of the few hairs which have clung to my head fall out but there is a new bristly growth underneath. My eyebrows and lashes are almost non-existent which makes me look incredibly weird. Why should the loss of such small amounts of hair have such a dramatic effect? I draw in my eyebrows but am never satisfied that they look OK. I also realise how important a job eyelashes perform – just as things sting my face when it's windy, they also go into my eyes.

On Tuesday February 10 Roy and I take our first (and probably last) steps towards stardom. We have been asked to appear in a video for Ovacome, the ovarian cancer support group. We go by train to Sloane Square and decide to go straight to the hotel where the filming is taking place. We intend to find the hotel then go window shopping until it is time for us to perform. However, when we arrive, Jenny Agutter, patron of Ovacome, is recording her section and we are invited to watch to see what goes on. We end up staying to watch for a couple of hours as the process is so fascinating.

We then meet the other three patients who are participating. They have all finished their treatment some time ago so it's good to meet women who are still clear and healthy after one or two years. I am very nervous about appearing on film but feel that if it can help others who have recently been diagnosed, then it is worthwhile. Roy and I are interviewed together and just have to answer questions about our reactions to the diagnosis, and treatment, our feelings about the future etc.

We leave the hotel around 5 o'clock – just the time to catch the rush-hour on the trains. We decide to look around the area and go for a pizza before setting off home. We miss our train connection at Richmond and at that point I realise how tired I am. It's been a long day and this is yet another reminder that I'm not back to full fitness.

On Thursday February 19 we have another visit to Hammersmith hospital to see Clare Wurr, Dr Thomas's research assistant who will explain the drug trial mentioned earlier. I will start with another laparoscopy to check whether or not I am clear of tumours. If I am clear I will be eligible for the treatment but will have only a one in three chance of having the drug – the other two in three are the control group. If any remaining tumour is found I will not be eligible but will not necessarily receive any treatment for the tumour straight away. This means that there is the possibility that I will just have to live with the knowledge that there is some disease left, that it could be growing and spreading – but Clare does say that plenty of people are knowingly living with tumours and able to live quite normally. However, it can't be easy and maybe ignorance is bliss.

I decide I will go ahead and take the chance that I may find out something I'd rather not know. The date is fixed for March 10 at the Hammersmith.

My hair starts to grow noticeably but not enough to abandon the wig. All through my treatment people have said how brave I've been – mainly, I suspect, because I haven't whinged too much – but I don't feel brave at all. To me, bravery means choosing to do something you find difficult or frightening. I haven't had a choice (except the choice of giving up or facing the treatment which I don't really regard as any choice at all – the survival instinct is very strong). The really brave thing I could have done would have been not to wear a wig at all but to face the world hairless. However, being the sort of person who prefers to blend into the background, I hide under my synthetic mop.

We leave home early on March 10 to be at the hospital by 9am. The traffic is horrendous but we get there soon after 9 expecting that I will be waiting around all morning anyway so a few minutes won't make too much difference. After booking in I reach my room and very soon find out that I am due to go to theatre almost immediately. My details are taken. One of the questions I am asked is how I feel about the operation – am I nervous? The nurse agrees it's a pretty silly question! I change into the usual stylish gown and I'm off with no time to sit and worry. I know that when I come round, if I have a tube sticking out of my abdomen I will have received the 'magic bullet'.

Back in my room I wake up and try to feel whether or not there is a tube, but, not wanting to poke around too hard, I can't tell. I soon know – everything is clear, but I am in the control group. The word 'remission' is used. So, although I am not to receive the experimental drug, there is no tumour to be found at least for now. I am able to go home in the afternoon – rather sore but not sorry to be let out.

It's a great relief to have the stitches out a week later – the tiny cut is exactly on my waist so everything I wear rubs it. Getting rid of the stitches immediately cures the problem.

THE 'C' WORD

The last weekend in March, we go to Madrid for a few days. We walk around the city for hours and I seem to have hardly less stamina than, say, a year ago, before the traumas all started. Back in our hotel room late Sunday afternoon, I feel a bit queasy. I'm soon overtaken by a violent bout of sickness and diarrhoea. This is very unusual for me and I wonder if the treatment has had some long-lasting effect making me more susceptible to such problems. Probably not. It's most likely to be 'something I ate' – but I suspect that for some time to come, whenever I have the slightest ailment I shall wonder if it's related to the big C.

By Monday, I'm pretty well recovered and we go walking in the Retro Park and the Botanical Gardens. It's sunny and soon very hot. I decide the time has come to expose my sparse thatch to the world and, out of the view of the public, I take off the wig. (I'm prepared to appear almost bald in a country where nobody knows me but I can't inflict the sight of a middle-aged woman actually taking her hair off on anyone, even total strangers!)

Tuesday April 7 is the day of the next check up with Dr Thomas following the tests at the Hammersmith. I'm feeling a bit twitchy as I know I will in the run-up to any future check-up. However well I feel I shall worry until I have the blood test result. On this occasion all is well. We know that the laparoscopy showed nothing that shouldn't be there but further tests have confirmed this and my CA125 count is about 8. Hilary Thomas is very pleased and the word 'cure' is even mentioned.

The next day we meet up with friends for lunch and I leave my wig off. I still feel very self-conscious and do feel that people are looking at me. I wonder if people think I just have a really freaky haircut or if they associate it with illness.

Eventually, I abandon the wig altogether and people are very complimentary – but then I suppose they would be. No-one is likely to say I look awful!

I reach a major milestone on May 11 – I play badminton exactly a year after giving up with my 'strained ribs and shoulder'. Some months before I was feeling that I wasn't making much progress, so Roy set me the challenge of playing again within the year. Even within a few weeks of the crucial date I didn't think I'd make it, but I did and without any apparent ill effects.

We have booked a holiday in Turkey – we leave on June 14 but two days before departure I develop a pain in my shoulder. I don't really think there is anything sinister about it but can't help remembering how this whole thing started.

We have a wonderful holiday but the pain persists – my thumb and first finger are numb at the tips and my arm keeps tingling. I hope that swimming might improve it but actually makes it worse.

The day after we get back from holiday we go to a studio in London to join Jenny Agutter and Debbie Howells in a series of radio interviews – some live broadcasts, others to be recorded for broadcasting at a later date. It's another very interesting day. Some interviewers are well-informed, others show their ignorance and lack of preparation by asking questions like 'What happens when you catch ovarian cancer?' as if it's something you pick up by sitting in a draught!

On Thursday July 9 I go back to see the chiropractor I consulted last year – he seems to be the best person to consult about my shoulder pain. He suggests that it could be caused by residual toxins following the chemotherapy. I have treatment over the next few weeks and the discomfort gradually goes away – unlike last year's problems.

He also suggests that I consult Raj, a homeopathic specialist. I do so a few days later. Raj has great difficulty finding anything wrong with me. I appear to be disgustingly healthy.

July 21 is my next check-up with Hilary Thomas – another twitchy few days while I wonder how the CA125 will be. It's 3.6 – extremely low – a great relief again. She does caution that feeling OK is no guarantee that all is well. The CA125 count can become quite elevated before any symptoms are experienced. However, for now, I am fine and she doesn't need to see me for another 4 months.

FULL CIRCLE

August 15. This journal has to stop sometime and one year after diagnosis seems to be a good time. It hasn't been a good year on the whole. On the other hand I feel absolutely fine now and it seems hard to believe it ever really happened. Those months of uncertainty, the chemo, the operations now seem long past. I'm very lucky to have responded so well to the treatment without the side effects being to traumatic. I know the recurrence rate of ovarian cancer is high but I can't spend my life worrying about the fact that it could come back. I have far more important things to worry about such as how do I cope with this curly hair after 50 years of dead straight locks!

I'm still very hesitant about producing this book and sending our story out into the public domain. I've been very lucky with the mildness of the side-effects of the chemo and would not want to suggest that others can depend on getting through it so easily. I have had private treatment so cannot comment on how different things would be with the NHS.

However, as we found such a shortage of information about ovarian cancer, perhaps the book might just give some help and encouragement to those who are newly diagnosed, as well as increasing awareness of the early signs.

During the past year many people have asked me how I felt when I first had the diagnosis. It's a difficult question to answer. In a way I feel that my reaction was not as strong as I might have predicted. No anger, no bitterness, no "Why me?" and certainly no "How long have I got, doctor?". I think I always regarded the cancer as a disease to be treated and cured like any other illness rather than something I was going to die of. Perhaps I was just burying my head in the sand – I really don't know. I can only say that this approach, together with complete openness and willingness to talk about the situation, is what worked for me.

ROY'S JOURNAL

HOW THINGS CAN CHANGE

May 1997 – Before Brittany

Linda mentions she has pains at the back of her right shoulder and lower right ribs. She thinks it is probably a strain from playing badminton. I don't take too much notice but in hindsight I reckon that since she rarely complains the pains must have been quite troublesome. She felt that our holiday in Brittany would provide an opportune break from badminton and allow the injury to mend.

May – After Brittany

It doesn't. The pains persist and, again in hindsight, it was also around this time that she became aware that she was putting on inches around the waist. Clothes which had fitted for years suddenly became difficult to fasten.

During the early hours of Tuesday 27 May Linda wakes up with severe pains below her ribs on the right hand side. I phone an emergency number to seek advice. A doctor phones back after about twenty minutes and talks to Linda. She recommends either going to casualty or waiting to make an urgent appointment first thing. Although it is very painful Linda does not fancy going to casualty at five thirty in the morning. She manages to see Dr Parry-Williams who thinks it most likely to be gall-bladder/gall-stones. This had been my inexpert view for some time as the shoulder/rib pain combination are classic symptoms. We book an ultra sound scan for the following day at the Princess Margaret. The pains have by then subsided.

Wednesday 28 May

Ultra sound scan

Dr Liyanage (Mrs) carries out the scan. The gall bladder shows no abnormalities. A chest X-ray shows some faint shadow. Dr L feels that the cause of the pain may be a pleurisy. Back to Dr Dalton, who prescribes antibiotics.

June/July

Loosening belts / shifting pains

The antibiotics fail to alleviate the pains although there has been no repeat of the acute attack. Linda's swelling continues and the pains begin to shift lower in the abdomen, sometimes to the side, sometimes central. Steadily she becomes more weary with the swelling and pains, and loses her appetite for food.

Dr Dalton expresses himself at a loss and refers Linda to Dr Sassoon (Sass) Levi, – consultant physician and gastro-enterologist. Dr Levi turns out to be on holiday – more delay and uncertainty.

Sunday 27 July

Black vomit

Tim and Tory came to dinner the previous evening. During the Sunday morning Linda feels suddenly nauseous and brings up a quantity of black vomit. Unusual both for the appearance and also because Linda very very rarely vomits. I feel OK but she checks with T&T just to make sure that it is nothing associated with the food. We never do establish the precise cause but, once more in hindsight, we think it was almost certainly something to do with her worsening condition.

I THINK WE NEED SOME HELP

Tuesday 29 July

Dr Levi

We have our consultation with Dr Levi, a charming man, probably late thirties.

Linda hands him a copy of an aide memoire she has prepared.

Age: 50

Non-smoker

Moderate drinker – not in excess of 14 unit per week guideline.

In early May I had pains in my right ribs and shoulder. I assumed this was a muscular problem from playing badminton and that, as I was about to go on holiday and not play badminton for a couple of weeks, it would probably go away. It did not, but was controlled by painkillers.

On our return from holiday, on May 26 I spent the day gardening and was aware of a sharp pain below my right ribs on bending. The next morning I awoke with an intense pain in the same place. My GP suggested that I could have a gall-bladder problem but a scan showed nothing. However, a chest X-ray showed a slight shadow and pleurisy was diagnosed. Antibiotics had no effect. Since then, that pain has diminished but it still hurts if pressed, and if I lie flat on my back, I feel that something is pressing upwards from under my ribs.

From that time I gradually developed tenderness around my waist. Initially it just hurt when anything pressed on it but now the pain is almost constant. Clothes which have fitted comfortably for years became tight and now I cannot do my clothes up – I have definitely grown around the middle although my weight stays fairly constant, and I feel bloated.

> *In the last couple of weeks I have developed diarrhoea, especially in the mornings. The motions are very soft and cause pain. I am also having pain on passing water and need to go two or three times during the night.*
>
> *I am becoming increasingly tired by the pain and have little energy. I have been unable to play badminton since May.*
>
> *On Sunday I vomited several times and, although this has stopped, I am still not eating normally.*

He questions Linda and then peers up her bottom. He sees nothing abnormal and asks her to come back at 0730 on Saturday August 2 for a colonoscopy. She must prepare for it by keeping to a prescribed diet from Thursday through to Friday pm, and then taking a powerful purgative and a cleansing fluid over the course of Friday afternoon. She must then fast until the process is complete.

Friday 1 August

Clean as a whistle

While I am at Gwenda's helping out with Talking Newspapers Linda returns home from work and proceeds to flush her system out as instructed. She does not like it!

Saturday 2 August

Colonoscopy/Gastroscopy

We arrive at the Thames Nuffield at 0730 and Linda is shown to her room. I leave her to the mercies of Dr Levi and return around lunch time to find her still very dozy – she only had an IV apparently but Linda is very easy to 'knock out' – as we once discovered with our home-made elderberry wine!

When Dr Levi appears he tells her that not only did he carry out a colonoscopy but he performed a gastroscopy as well (jokes about cleaning the tube after the former are usual at this juncture in the story). He tells Linda that he had to ask her permission before proceeding but Linda can recall absolutely nothing about either process – lucky her!

Dr Levi has seen nothing abnormal in the colon but her oesophagus is much inflamed, so much so that he was not prepared to take biopsy samples. He also reports that Linda is carrying a large amount of fluid in her stomach which should not be there. (He actually said 'stomach' and we are both misled at this point. In fact, he meant the abdominal – or peritoneal – cavity.) He tells Linda that the fluid must be drained and analysed. He wants her to take antacid capsules (Zoton) to reduce the inflammation of the oesophagus.

We make yet another appointment – at the Paragon Suite in Wexham – for the following Wednesday afternoon, 6 August. She will need an overnight stay and she will have the drain inserted shortly after arrival. An ultra sound scan will be carried out prior to the drain being inserted and a CAT scan is programmed for the Thursday am.

Monday 4 August

Ascites/Helen's learned books

Dr Levi sends Linda a copy of a letter he has written to Dr Dalton. He describes Linda as 'charming'. He raises the matter of the fluid and refers to it as 'ascites'. Linda and I consult Helen's medical reference books and Edward's medical dictionary. Oops! Neither of us like what we read – although I think I probably spent rather longer reading about all the possibilities than Linda did. Apparently the appearance of the fluid (yellow, clear, milky etc) may be indicative of the cause. Causes include cirrhosis of the liver, malignancy – of liver or ovaries, or heart conditions. None sound very encouraging. I can't imagine that Linda has cirrhosis as she drinks moderately – unlike me – but perhaps there are other causes for it. I settle for cirrhosis as sounding marginally less unpleasant than cancer.

Wednesday 6 August

Ascitic drain/CAT

We arrive at the Paragon Suite on the Wednesday afternoon, around three o'clock, and Linda is taken down to the theatre to have the drain inserted. Very painful, she reports later. Dr Charig tells her as he inserts it through the abdominal wall that she will yell. She does. I return home while this is going on to fetch Linda's slippers. It is a filthy wet afternoon.

When I return she is attached to a tube and a bag. The bag is filling rapidly. I call a nurse to replace it. She seems unfamiliar with the process and after a further twenty minutes or so we have to call again as the bag has filled yet again. The nurse measures the volumes after a fashion and we later estimate that, including the fluid which drained in the theatre, the total ascitic fluid generated is in excess of three litres. Three kilos! Half a stone! What a great way to lose weight! The rate of flow subsides and I leave Linda for the night.

Next Day

I return to collect Linda. She has the scan at around nine thirty. Again the nursing staff appear unsure of what is expected of them and Linda has to remind them early on that she must take a dye in order for the scan to be effective. Scan complete and drain removed we head home. Linda has had a very uncomfortable night – hardest bed she has ever slept in and she spent some of the night sitting in a chair. The great thing though is that she feels such relief after the removal of all that fluid. What does it all mean though?

Friday 8 August

Puzzling analysis

Dr Levi telephones. Linda is at work but he is happy to talk to me. He has had the result of the CAT scan. Nothing showed up. That's good, I suggest. No tumour. But Dr Levi cautions that the analysis of the ascitic fluid is 'puzzling'. He wants to repeat the gastroscopy – this time to remove biopsy samples and he wants to introduce Linda to Mr Desai, a surgeon who will perform a laparoscopy, and possibly a laparotomy, a few days later. The appointment for the gastroscopy is made for the following Tuesday. I mention the fact that it is our 30th wedding anniversary and Dr Levi sounds genuinely apologetic. I agree though that the show must go on so we arrange to take Linda into the Thames Nuffield around eleven o'clock .

Tuesday 12 August

Repeat gastroscopy

Once again Linda appears to have slept through the procedure, the thought of which makes me want to gag. Dr Levi appears and tells Linda that he has been able to take plenty of biopsy samples. Mr Desai will appear at some point. The sister in charge advises that Mr Desai will be around until eight o'clock. As we had hoped to celebrate our anniversary that evening we ask if we could see him earlier. On our own we decide that in any event it might be prudent to postpone our celebration until the following evening. I phone the restaurant to rearrange. Dr Levi and Mr Desai appear at around six thirty. Mr Desai is a tall, rather serious man who explains what he will do. He stresses that at this stage all he intends to do is exploratory, take lots of biopsy samples, hopefully by laparoscopy alone but as he may need to investigate further he will seek Linda's prior permission to continue to perform the more severe operation without having to subject her to a further anaesthetic in a few days time. He confirms Dr Levi's observation about the analysis of the ascites. He says it revealed 'suspicious cells'.

DARK DAYS AND MORE FRUSTRATION

Friday 15 August

Arrive at hospital around 1620. Linda has had laparoscopy and laparotomy. In great pain, drip into left wrist. Moisten her mouth with swab. Nurse tells me there is a phone call. Dr Levi waiting outside. Although no tumours showed on the scan, or by colonoscopy/gastroscopy, Mr Desai has found tumours on her intestine. It has spread. It is INOPERABLE. Does that mean? – yes, chemotherapy. How long? – depends how she FIGHTS it. I tell Dr Levi that Linda is keen badminton player, very competitive. Dr Levi assures me that that is an advantage. He says they can do things about the pain. What pain? I wonder. Does he mean terminal pain? Or, just for now?

Mr Desai comes in and tells it from his angle. He has found a tumour and cannot remove it because it would damage the blood supply to the bowel. Don't really understand but it does nothing to lighten the dark cloud which is forming in my mind – and possibly Linda's, although she is still hazy after the anaesthetic.

She is in severe pain, but wants me to go to see her mother – better than over the phone. I don't think Win really follows (later that night she rings me at home to ask how Linda is and I have only seen her, Win, a few hours ago).

I think I spoke to Dave at some point. Can't be sure. I am very confused, muddled.

Saturday 16 August

A restless night. Get up around seven and reach hospital just after eight. Linda is in desperate pain. Give her more swab to suck. She has had five doses of morphine during the night and she is still acutely aware of the pain. Eventually, a combination of morphine and pethedine is tried. Whoopee. It seems to work. Amazing improvement. She is washed and allowed to sit up in a chair. Lots of pillows for padding. She is more comfortable but weak. Mr Desai calls in and confirms that he will be advising a Dr Ashford – Oncologist – of Linda's condition. He says that he – Mr Desai – could, if necessary, bypass the tumour but Linda would still be able to eat and drink normally and have use of her bowel. So, not a bag, as far as we can tell. However, she is not at that stage and hopefully it will not reach it if the chemotherapy takes effect.

I go home and do some chores and I manage to contact one of Edward's scouting colleagues to get the message to Ed that I want to see him as soon as he returns from camp. He appears a short while later while I am in the vegetable garden and I break the news to him. He does not say much but I guess it is as difficult for him to grasp as it was for me when I first heard. After he has left I plough my way through the remains of Tuesday night's curry which we put in the freezer. Normally I enjoy such leftovers and I even fry some courgettes to go with it but I am really just eating because I feel I ought to. Tim phones while I am eating. He says that they are devastated by the news. I return to the hospital about six o'clock. She is still sitting, relieved of the acute pain. She is now drinking water – but still on the drip. It is very hot so they are concerned about dehydration. I help her to the loo several times and sponge her face. She likes the cool water evaporating off her face. She is allowed consommé and jelly for supper. Yummy. No solids allowed until she farts. I stay with her until ten. She does not want to return to bed because lying down hurts but the nurses sort her out and she later tells me that she was helped into bed around midnight. Around the same time I am also dropping into an uneasy sleep back home.

Alan Burn phones not long after I get home and we have a long chat. Like everyone I have told he and Bridget are utterly gob-smacked.

Sunday 17 August

Arrive at the hospital around eight forty five. She is much brighter, sitting watching TV and looking at the newspaper. The drip is still attached but she has been told it can be removed. She has had more consommé and jelly for breakfast, the rule being: no farts, no solids. Eventually the drip is removed and she is free to wander without her 'zimmer'. We go for a stroll in the grounds. She finds the open air a great relief – it is still less than 48 hours since the knife but she is much improved. Mr Desai phones in and is satisfied at what the nurses tell him. No farts though.

Dr Levi visits, bringing his two year old son Benjamin. They usually hunt for golf balls on a Sunday morning. I think Linda is cheered by the kind attention from the doctors and nursing staff.

I stay with her for lunch and then go home for a while. I return early evening and we watch 'Antiques Hunt', 'Pie in the Sky', and 'Jewel in the Crown'. I leave her just after ten. I pour myself a generous scotch, cock up the end of the recording of 'The Sculptress' and take my 'Language – The Basics' book up to bed to read. I wake at 0045 still sitting up in bed with my book open and my glass in my hand.

Monday 18 August

0715. I should have been at Gatwick, en route to Tobago, but I am dusting the lounge instead. Linda phones to tell me she has farted. I finish my chores, have some breakfast and hurry off to the hospital. Linda has appraised Mr Desai of her success and he has told her she can order proper breakfast and lunch and then go home. We spend the morning reading the papers, watching telly and walking about. I go across the road to the Plough for a beer and prawn sandwich. While I am eating the sandwich in the garden I hear the occasional faint 'click' and from time to time I am aware of things falling to the ground. On investigation I find that seed pods on a cluster of caper spurge plants are drying and bursting, showering the garden with seeds.

We finally leave the hospital around three thirty.

Tuesday 19 August

We spend the day quietly and have a sleep in the afternoon. We have arranged for a chap to come at seven o'clock to arrange Enduring Powers of Attorney for both of us, with Edward also named. He and Nicola will then stay on for a BBQ. This thing – Linda's illness – has concentrated the mind on what one ought to be doing to arrange one's affairs more sensibly. OK, hopefully we don't need to use the EPoA but at least it's out of the way. We will also check whether our Wills are still correct.

About half past six Mr Desai phones to ask us both to go and see him to discuss the results. Linda starts to explain that we have visitors etc., but I tell her that we will go. She agrees to see Mr Desai soon after eight o'clock. This gives us time in fact to see our EPoA chap, and to delegate the BBQ effort to Edward.

Arrive at the hospital fearing yet more bad news. It is though rather better than we expected. Mr Desai believes the tumour started in an ovary and although it has spread he states that the response of ovarian cancer to chemotherapy is very good. Quite what this means in respect of the tumour on the bowel is not clear but it certainly sounds more encouraging. Mr Desai will now refer Linda to Dr Richard Ashford, a top cancer specialist. Unfortunately he is on holiday and we will not have an appointment until after 1 September. Yet more waiting. I ask Mr Desai what impact attitude has on the success of the treatment. His response is unequivocal – it is a key factor. Whilst I know Linda must be very worried and frightened, I know also how positive and determined she is in terms of everything she does and I think she has a very strong chance of getting through this illness. OK, life will never quite be the same. We will tend to look over our shoulders, and there is always the risk that it could return. But I think it will strengthen the bonds between us and may well enrich our lives even after thirty years of marriage.

Tuesday 20 August

We go for a chat with Dr Dalton, at his request (or Dr Levi's). He is most concerned and more or less admits that he failed to recognise the ascites. I then take Linda to the Nuffield for the blood sample. We now wait for the results. Linda is making a list of questions to ask Mr Desai when we next see him. He has seen the 'Thing' so what does it look like? How big is it? How long has it been there?

We fix another appointment with Mr Desai.

Thursday 22 August

We are due to see Mr Desai this evening but he calls to postpone it as he wants the results of the CA125 analysis – the marker for ovarian cancer.

Tuesday 26 August

The grief of others

Linda fancies a walk so we select one of the reasonably gentle and well described ones from our Thames Valley Pub Walks book. We park near the 'Spade Oak' between Bourne End and Marlow and follow the sketch map along the Thames, across the Marlow Donkey railway line and then along a path by some gravel pits. Somewhere towards the end of the walk Linda points out that we have strayed from the public footpath and have ended up in someone's back garden. A group of people are sitting and standing beneath the trees. It all appears very tranquil. "I'm sorry," I say, "But are we on your land?" A woman in a black dress walks over to us. "Yes, you are," she replies, "But don't worry, everybody does it." She pauses. And then, with a tremor in her voice she continues "My husband didn't believe in fences." Another pause. Her eyes fill with tears. "Sorry," she says, "He died last Friday. My daughter as well. On a motor bike in the Heathrow tunnel at one thirty in the morning. No one else involved. He didn't drink."

What do you say? I feel her remorse. It is dreadful. But she is brave enough to face us, with dignity, and even with humour. I mutter something crass about Linda's tumour –

somewhere in there, pointing to her abdomen – but, really, when you are faced with such raw finality, what should you say?

Friday 29 August

We have another consultation with Mr Desai. He confirms that the CA125 level is high which suggests strongly that the ovarian cancer theory is correct. Linda runs through her questions. It appears that the cancer lies on the surface of the bowel, completely surrounding it, and it has covered the omentum, the fatty apron lining the wall of the abdomen. There is some on the surface of the liver. How long it has been developing it is impossible to say, as no one really knows the rate of doubling in any particular instance. Mr Desai tells Linda to keep smiling. Both he and Dr Levi seem to have high regard for her plucky spirit – which augers well.

This is a special day for other reasons. Helen is due to return today. Although Linda knows that Helen will cut her travels short she does not know until six o'clock that Helen is due to arrive in Heathrow at 1835 this evening from Sydney via Rome on Alitalia Flight No. AZ208. When Linda arrives home from work I am tuned into the flight arrival times on Ceefax on one TV, while she sips her tea and watches 'Neighbours' on another, oblivious to my restiveness. Helen's flight is alone in having no current information whatsoever associated with it. No EST, no delay, no nothing. It is as if it does not exist. Calls to BAA and Alitalia are a waste of time. They simply have recorded messages advising scheduled departures and arrivals. I have to assume all will be well though and I decide to break it to Linda that Helen is on her way. Soon. Ish. I tell Linda that the food she has asked me to get ready (for the two of us) is not enough for five. She looks quizzical. "Well," I explain, "Edward and Nicola are coming over *(pause for effect)* after we pick Helen up at Heathrow." I will never forget Linda's expression at that moment. Disbelief was rapidly followed by sheer delight.

Eventually I get through to someone sensible at Heathrow and am advised that Helen's plane has landed, about twenty minutes late. To the best of our knowledge it never featured on the Ceefax screen for that day. By the time we arrive at Heathrow Helen has cleared Customs and is looking out for us. As we pass through the Heathrow tunnel I remember the woman in black and we tell Helen the sad story. One recent and almost personal tragedy. For us, a wonderful day. A great tonic for Linda. What a strange lottery life is.

Sunday 31 August

Death of a Princess

I go down stairs to make tea a few minutes later than usual. By the time I turn on the kitchen radio the Radio 4 News is about halfway through and it takes a while for me to understand what has actually happened. When I return to the bedroom with the tray I tell Linda the sad news. Over the rest of that day our own problems for a while get pushed into the background as the realisation of the terrible accident that claimed the life of 'The Peoples' Princess' sinks in.

Tuesday 2 September

At last, our appointment with Dr Ashford. Booked for 2015 we eventually get to see him at 2145. As soon as we realise it is going to be along wait I return home for victuals – two bananas – and a BUPA form which we had forgotten.

Alas! Dr Ashford examines Linda and agrees the ovarian cancer diagnosis BUT he specialises in breast cancer and believes it more appropriate to refer her to another specialist – Dr Hilary Thomas. He assures us that the delay is not critical – but Linda is now getting anxious to receive treatment – I feel the same, but try to be as reassuring as I can.

Thursday 4 September

We are both beginning to feel frustrated by the delays and I reason that by the time Dr Ashford has formally briefed Dr Thomas and she has then made contact with us more valuable time will be lost. In an attempt to move things along faster I manage to track down Hilary Thomas's secretary at the Princess Margaret only to be told that her diary is fully booked for the following Tuesday, her day at Princess Margaret (9 September) and then she is at a conference in Germany for two weeks. I explain the background to her secretary, who sounds really sympathetic. She promises to ring back. Linda takes the call. Great. We have an appointment for 9 September, 1030, but we must ensure all paperwork is forwarded. Linda hopes that chemotherapy can start asap after that appointment.

We then contact Dr Ashford's secretary, Mr Desai's secretary, and Dr Levi's secretary to inform, request and cajole.

PROGRESS AT LAST

Tuesday 9 September

Linda receives a copy of a letter Dr Levi has written to Dr Thomas. Linda is now not only 'charming' but 'intelligent' as well.

We see Dr Thomas – punctually – at the Princess Margaret. She is a dynamic and impressive young woman. She explains the treatment that Linda will have – assuming the ovarian origin is finally confirmed. Dr Thomas wants to make absolutely sure and will review all the data before finally committing herself to the course of treatment. Apparently the CA125 marker is high but not enormously so. Assuming it is ovarian Linda will have three sessions of chemo using carboplatin AND taxol. She will lose her hair because of the taxol but the drug has been shown to lengthen the life expectancy over that for the traditional drugs when used on their own.

After three sessions – spaced at twenty one day intervals – Linda will have surgery, at the Hammersmith or the Wellington – to remove ovaries etc and any other tissue that can be removed. She will spend a week in hospital. Following that the chemotherapy programme will be repeated.

Linda will have to go for a kidney function assessment at the Hammersmith within the next few days. That is to establish – together with her weight and height – the optimal dose levels for the chemo.

Thursday 11 September

Appointment at the Hammersmith 1130. We go first to imaging department for an injection of radioactive tracer. That takes about half an hour after which we wander off for lunch. Find a delightful country pub (pretty grotty actually but the only one in sight!) and have sandwich/ploughman's before going back to have half hourly blood samples taken at the cancer centre, which is a fairly new development at Hammersmith. Not particularly traumatic for Linda, just a bit boring. We do see a lot of cancer sufferers wandering around looking thin/ bald / ill. We return home by around 1615 – in time for Countdown.

Saturday 13 September

My Birthday!

The previous afternoon I booked a night in a hotel in Canterbury for tonight. Linda – and I – fancied a break. We drive down and arrive around noon. Very pleasant hotel and room. We potter around the town and look at the cathedral. All very beautiful. Buy a couple of books in Waterstones. One is the Encyclopaedia of the English Language by David Crystal, which Linda gives me as an additional birthday present. The other book is the Poet's Manual and Rhyming Dictionary. I am not particularly keen on poetry – reading or writing it – but I am interested in metre, and rhythm.

Back in the room we relax and make love. Afterwards we watch Blind Date before going to Sully's, the Hotel restaurant. We have a lovely meal and a quick walk around the block to get us ready for sleep. Not too bad a night until I am woken by clicking pipes – at least that's what I think it was. I can't investigate because I don't want to wake Linda.

Sunday 14 September

We get up late and pig out on a full English Breakfast. We finally depart around 1030 and head for Whitstable. We park near the harbour and walk to shingle beach. After that we decide to press on to Herne Bay. Nice. Then drive further east along the coast to Reculver. Again very pleasant but nowhere to eat. We only want a snack so we decide to head back westwards past Herne Bay to Whitstable. I fancy some oysters but the only two places we can find are full and smoky. We try Faversham, but only full Sunday lunch served so we decide to head home. Eventually we have a sandwich and fizzy drink at the service area on the M25!

Nevertheless it has been a jolly nice weekend and Linda seems to have enjoyed it.

Wednesday 24 September

CHEMODAY!!!

I drop Linda off at the Princess Margaret Hospital at ten o'clock and go into Slough to buy odds and sods. Pass Sabino and no one waiting so decide to get my haircut. Arrive back at PMH around ten past eleven. Linda is connected up to the drip (Taxol first) and is chatting to Lorraine and a pretty Belgian nurse, Sabine, who is shadowing Lorraine. There had been difficulty in inserting the cannula and Linda has bruises on her left hand where they tried first before getting the RMO to try her right hand (successful). Kath Johnson pops in for a visit and chats for a while. A women comes to take our lunch order. Linda goes for soup, quiche and pudding. I, abstemious as always, have tomato juice and prawn sandwich. The Taxol drips in slowly – about three hours because of its viscosity. At two o'clock, the drip is changed to the carboplatin after a brief flush with saline.

By three fifteen it's over and we leave. Time seems to have passed quickly and Linda feels OK.

Weekend 27/28 September

We don't plan anything for this weekend because Linda could feel side-effects from the chemo – flu-like, achy symptoms, etc. In the event, she does not have anything more than a few aches in her legs on the Saturday evening. However she is experiencing a lot of discomfort in her abdomen around the middle.

Wednesday 1 October

I take Linda for blood test at PMH. We have a chat with Lorraine. Apparently the discomfort is unlikely to be a side-effect from the chemo. We will perhaps try to arrange consultation with Hilary Thomas if it persists/ worsens.

Thursday 9 October

A cluster of Linda's pubic hair comes away in my fingers as we make love. The moult has begun. She says her scalp is sore and her eyebrows itch. It is only a matter of time before her head hair starts to fall. She is rather depressed.

Friday 10 October – Sunday 12 October

We take a weekend break in the New Forest, staying a little way north of Lyndhurst in very pleasant country hotel – though hardly the 'Luxury' category claimed in the brochure blurb.

Linda begins to lose the hair from her head.

We have an energetic and enjoyable session on the Friday morning before going down to breakfast. Linda's condition has not affected that aspect of our lives – at least not yet – although she is aware of some brief discomfort after orgasm. After a quick breakfast we hit the road.

The New Forest – Lyndhurst, Lymington, Brockenhurst, Milford-on-Sea, Barton-on-Sea, Burley – is a joy. All very pretty.

On the Sunday we stop off at Southampton, and then drive on to Fareham to have lunch with Kim Harry. All in all it has been a very pleasant weekend – although Linda is not terribly happy about the hair loss.

Wednesday 15 October

Things proceed much the same as the first session. We chat and read. We see Hilary Thomas before leaving. Linda's CA125 level (on blood sample taken on 8 October) shows good drop in proportion to initial sample (100 v 257). Hilary gives us Mr McIndoe's telephone number so we can to fix a consultation. She predicts surgery is likely to be during w/c 17 November.

The hair loss is gathering pace. It is no longer a matter of peering at the pillow to see a few strays, now it falls out in great clumps. The wig will soon be needed.

Thursday 16 October

Linda goes to work!! And that after very disturbed night – not entirely my fault although apparently I did snore a bit. It was the same last time – she had a sleepless night after the chemo. L complains (no she doesn't) reports pain in upper left chest on walking, pinkness, and pains in abdomen. Again, it is all much the same as after the first treatment.

Friday 17 October

Drive up to Trevor and Elaine's and have a pub lunch. Before we depart for Solihull to pick up my father Linda puts the wig on for its first outing. She says nothing to Dad and eventually we tell him that she has it on. He suspected she must be wearing it in view of my comments about the hair loss but he maintains that he cannot tell that it is a wig.

Wednesday 22 October

The hair loss is very advanced. She still has eyebrows and lashes but little left on her head. She clearly feels self conscious but it really isn't so bad. For appearances in public the wig is fantastic. It fools Dr Dalton, it really is good, you just cannot tell. She wears a bandana in the house if others are around but she will get used to the baldness in time. I take photos with and without wig before she leaves for work.

Thursday 23 October

Linda asks me to use my beard trimmer to tidy the straggly remains of her hair. It looks much better when I have done it.

"THERE IS NO CURE"

Friday 24 October

We drive up to the Hammersmith for a consultation with Mr McIndoe. He turns out to be a good-looking, quietly spoken man aged about forty. He has not received any papers about Linda so it is fortunate that we have taken along Dr Levi's letter to Hilary Thomas. He reads it and makes a few notes and then examines Linda. He expresses surprise at the laparotomy scar as he expected to see only the smaller laparoscopy incision. Apparently had he – Mr McIndoe – performed a laparotomy he would have removed more at the time. As it is, he explains why surgery to remove ovaries, uterus, cervix, omentum etc. etc., coupled with chemotherapy, is currently felt to offer the best in terms of life expectancy. He does caution quite bluntly though "There is no cure." I think we know that but it is a bit stark when put that way. He then comments that some people do survive for many years. He tells Linda the choice – surgery or no surgery – is hers, but then says that if it were his wife in that situation he would want her to have the operation.

So we agree to go ahead. Linda will go into the Wellington in St Johns Wood on November 24 – Edward's 25th birthday – and will be operated on the following day. She will spend up to ten days there and Mr McIndoe will remove as many of the tumour affected sites as possible.

Wednesday 5 November

Chemo-session number three

Chemo again follows the same procedure as the first two sessions. Blood samples are taken to check platelet level – OK. Then the pre-medication. First, 8mg of Zofran (ondansetron) an anti-emetic; very special, Lorraine tells us, as it is used by astronauts to combat the nausea caused by zero gravity. Second, 8mg of dexamethasone, a steroid to prevent systemic allergic reaction. Third, an anti colonergic, ranitidine, 50mg. And finally 4mg of Piriton (chlorpheniramine), an anti histamine drug. Linda will continue with the Zofran and dexamethasone in tablet form for a few days following the session.

The RMO inserts the cannula. He is the one Linda saw on the first occasion when Lorraine had difficulty finding a vein. He seems to have no problem and it is inserted very swiftly. Linda is left on a saline drip for quite a while before starting with the Taxol. However it is rather warm in the room so her blood vessels are dilated and we soon make up time. She finishes around three o'clock and Lorraine takes her to see a woman who has had the operation but who is only on her first chemo. Our final excitement for the afternoon is a trip to Tesco. Linda comments on a pain in her chest – upper left – as she walks. She felt it after earlier sessions and later discovers that it can be a side effect of the Zofran. "Report it to your doctor immediately," the blurb advises!

Thursday 6 November to Sunday 9 November

I go to Brussels and leave Linda to have a quiet weekend. I check up on her condition throughout and she reports that apart from some aches and twinges she does not feel any worse than on the first two occasions. The chest pain has gone but I think she should mention it to Lorraine at least.

The operation has been put back a couple of days – yet to be confirmed.

Tuesday 11 November

Linda has her dates confirmed. Enter The Wellington on Thursday 27 November at eleven o'clock. The operation is scheduled for three thirty the next day.

Thursday 13 November

We have a day out in Cheltenham. Beautiful town lots of walking. Linda buys us lunch at a Japanese restaurant – yummy. After lunch she goes off for an hour or so to do some

Christmas shopping while I potter around antique shops. She seems to be pretty well and we have a lovely day, returning home around seven o'clock after a rather tiring drive in the dark and rain.

Sunday 16 November

Linda has a cold but does not feel too bad. She does mention her irregular heart beat though. Every so many beats it misses one. Odd. She must not forget to mention this when she goes for her operation.

Wednesday Thursday 19/20 November

Linda's last blood test before the big op. She mentions the irregular heart beat to Lorraine who thinks that it is probably hormonal but suggests that Linda should mention it to Mr McIndoe. We go to the Fine Arts and Antiques Fair at Olympia which has some magnificent objects and paintings. Linda is somewhat put off by the fact that very little is affordable! I settle for a small dish by Omar Ramsden. Very pretty and something by one of the great British silversmiths. We saw some superb stuff by Omar Ramsden (and Alwyn Carr) at Fay Lucas's stand. A silver and enamelled box for £7500 was rather tempting but ....

Linda is pretty worn out by the time we arrived home – me too. She falls asleep after tea and snoreds away gently for half an hour or more. I think the diversion has been good though as the forthcoming op is occupying her (and my) mind more and more.

Tuesday 25 November

He does exist! The long-awaited lunch with 'Rog' (Creswell) takes place. We meet on the bridge between Eton and Windsor and head for Eton Wine Bar. The lunch is a success. Roger is his usual charming (where women are concerned!) self and Linda seems very relaxed. After Linda has left – to visit her Mum – Roger expresses his admiration for her. "She looks so well, matey." Or some such utterance. He then launches into the detailed chemistry of how cytotoxins – like carboplatin – actually work. As usual I show my ignorance and, as usual, Roger says, "Come on, matey, you're a f**kin' chemist." As usual, my protestations – "Long time ago", "Inorganic chemistry", "Never liked the subject, anyway" – butter few parsnips. To return to the main subject matter, notwithstanding Linda's lament at my condition when I eventually return home – "Yes, I thought he (Roger) was all right, until you come home like this" – inviting Linda along to lunch served the purpose of creating yet another diversion from the horrible events ahead.

Another shadow on the day – apart from my inebriation – is that when Linda arrives at Garrick House she finds that her Mum has been admitted to Wexham Park Hospital. Nothing acute but possibly a small stroke.

Thursday 27 November

Into the Time Warp

After breakfast we make love somewhat hastily then leave to travel up to The Wellington by train and Tube (and Tube) arriving almost to the minute at the stated admission time – 11 o'clock.

After registration we head for Room 661. Although, in theory, a 'B' scale, shared room, 661 has just one bed, bathroom, two chairs, TV (Sky Sport), fridge (small but with an ice box and big enough for a few bottles of Tonic) and a balcony (not much use in November, but nevertheless a balcony). This will be Linda's world – apart from her outing to the theatre and the ITU – for the next ten days. The drawers and cupboards will become familiar, she will master the idiosyncrasies of the soap dispenser, she will develop routines which suit her. Only news of the 'outside world' and visits from friends and family will disrupt those routines. Room 661 will be her personal Time Warp. She will survive.

A petite bronzed Oz nurse with a splendid chest takes Linda's details soon after entering the Warp.

Mr McIndoe visits briefly to check if Linda is OK and to ask if she has any questions. Why is one's mind always a blank at such times? She does at least remember to ask for a sample of tumour which causes Mr McIndoe to wrinkle his nose. Seems it is not a common request – blame it on John Diamond, we say. Anyway McI says he will try to save a bit.

Various other people arrive to ask questions, take samples and give information. We both have lunch – Linda's last solid food for some time.

A beautiful basket of flowers arrives from Kim and Heather.

Linda works at her tapestry. I spend most of the time trying – unsuccessfully – to complete the Times crossword.

I leave just before half past seven and head for Baker Street and home. A huge knot of anxiety and apprehension seems to fill my body. That is how it will be now until she is through the worst. In truth that is how it has been since August 15. I cannot concentrate on anything except her condition.

Friday 28 November

What's in store?

I wake early – 6 o'clock or so – as usual but doze off from time to time. Helen brings me a pot of tea and biscuits and goes off to work. I phone Linda. She has had a reasonable night but the 'Clean-prep' is working so she is dashing off to the loo quite often. Marta – our borrowed au pair – arrives on the dot of ten to do some cleaning. I go into Slough to bank Linda's pay cheque and get my hair cut. After 'Call My Bluff' I go out and plant some crocus corms in the trough outside the front door. Time ticks on slowly. I phone Linda from time to time usually about nothing in particular. She phones me at twenty to three to tell me she has been told to change into the hospital gown and get on to the bed. The scheduled time for the operation is three thirty. I try to switch off and busy myself with little things. I watch 'Countdown' which is jolly as always and a nice diversion but my score seems to get progressively worse each day. A guy called Ray McPhie, aged 53, is champion and he pronounces the 't' in 'Consonant, please Carol' almost as a separate word. "Consonan-Tuh", "Another consonan-Tuh."

Ros phones. Hrastan phones. I am not going to phone the hospital until six o'clock. I get through to Oz Nurse Christine of the Splendid Chest. Linda is in the Recovery Room and will be returning to 661 and not into ITU. "Is this good?" I ask. ON Christine-of-the-SC does not have an answer. She has merely been advised that Linda will be back in her charge sooner than planned. "Must be good," I muse, "Or have they just opened her up and decided there's nothing can be done." I settle for the former.

At around nine thirty when Edward, Nicola, Helen and Jamie are all with me the phone rings. A slightly slurred female voice says "Hello." It's Linda! She is very tired, very woozy, but it is great to hear her. She tells me she has a catheter but no drains – why? she wonders and she also wonders about the fact that she did not go into ITU. I think she is going down my latter route of reasoning.

"WE WERE VERY PLEASED"

Saturday 30 November

Post-op

I arrive at The Wellington just after eleven. Linda is sitting in a chair – vomiting. The flowers which I ordered earlier in Datchet have yet to arrive. I doubt that Linda is really too bothered that I have not brought any with me. Probably she has not even noticed. She has a drip in one arm, PCA in the other and a catheter. Considering what she has been through she looks remarkably good. A bit pale but her skin looks smooth and soft.

She apologises for being sleepy but I am happy just to be with her and to do what little I can to make her comfortable. She does point out that a tumour sample has been preserved as requested. It is disappointingly small and nondescript – an off-white blob of gristle sitting in a few drops of pink watery fluid. I don't suppose Linda will want to volunteer to provide a larger specimen.

The anaesthetist pops in and we have the first really good news we have had for months (OK, CA125 counts going down is good but ...). Apparently the operation was much more straightforward than she (the anaesthetist) or Mr McIndoe had anticipated – two hours as opposed to three and a half or four – and she was very clear inside. This explains why ITU was not needed nor the drains.

The flowers arrive: a crude posy of nondescript blooms and miscellaneous foliage which looks as if it has been plucked from a hedgerow in August after a long drought. Apologetically I conceal the label which associates it with me, so that visitors don't think me a tight-fisted old sod. Not long after a beautiful flower arrangement arrived. From

Groundwork Thames Valley. What wonderfully caring people they are. What a wonderfully super person Linda is. GTV have met her only once – and my involvement (with GTV) has been sporadic to say the least – but Linda matters to them. I really appreciate that.

I leave the hospital at six thirty. The knot in my chest feels a little looser. Is there a god? If so, "Thanks, mate."

While settling down for the night I remember that terribly sad encounter we had with the woman who had days before lost her husband and daughter in a motor bike accident near Heathrow. I make a note to include my recollections in this journal. (*vide supra*)

Sunday 30 November

Family reunion

I drive up with Edward and Helen. Linda is awake, sitting up, listening to 'The Archers' and announces that she has had a small breakfast. She has clearly improved overnight. We all have (very weak) coffee and chat. Edward and I pop out for a pub lunch while Helen assists Linda to eat hers. Linda takes a walk supported by Helen and one of two Irish Mary's on duty today. (ON Christine-of-the-SC turns up later – I am not sure if Edward shares my awe of the SC). We watch 'The Clothes Show', some Pop Awards thing later, and we all depart. I am so tired I am probably a hazard and just to prove it when we reach Nicola and Edward's place H and E tell me that I reversed into another (unoccupied) car while parking. I disagree. I think I simply entered a rut which caused the car to jolt. Both cars? No damage, anyway. At least so far as I can ascertain.

Monday 1 December

Arrive at The Wellington around ten thirty. Linda is looking still brighter. We wait for Mr McIndoe to put in an appearance but by half past three she is told that he will not be around until after five o'clock. At which point one of the nurses and I help Linda into the bath where she sits on a stool under the shower. Her dressing is removed revealing an enormous scar running from breast bone to pubic bone. After drying herself Linda dons a clean nightie, she puts on some earrings – the ones John Cox gave her – and make up, and puts her wig on. I find it difficult to believe that 72 hours before she had undergone major surgery.

I return home by six forty in time for a rushed sandwich which Helen has ready for me and the two of us go to Slough Writers' Group. Helen wins third prize in the article competition with her 'Priscilla Show – Imperial Hotel'. As usual I get nowhere although I got some laughs when I read out mine: 'An -ism for a dead cow'. Helen and I join a quiz downstairs in the bar but before it starts I phone Linda. Mr McIndoe has done his rounds and he confirms what the anaesthetist already told us – that the op was much more straightforward than they feared it might be. Virtually all the tumour has disappeared – the omentum had shrunk to the size – if balled up – of a plum. Linda's tumour sample is in fact from the omentum. She is told that she can leave around Friday if she feels up to it.

The quiz is a riot. Six in each team. Helen is our Captain. The Question Master is an absolute Toss-pot. Our teams wins. By between seven and ten points. Nobody knows exactly but our opponents concede that we won. A jolly good evening. In fact, a jolly good day all told.

Tuesday 2 December

On the way up to St John's Wood I stop off at Green Park and wander through to New Bond Street to get an opinion from Sotheby's about Linda's silver overlay vase which we bought in Namur. The expert believes it is French as it shows features associated with the St Louis works (Maltese cross type marks in the etching). Alternatively it could be American but still with the St Louis influence. About £300 he reckons (we paid the equivalent of £400 in Belgium – so what!)

Linda has had the catheter removed and she feels much more comfortable being able to pee naturally. Yet more flowers are delivered.

I have coffee with Linda by which time Helen arrives. I then go off for lunch with Victoria Le Suer of Brewin Dolphin to discuss investments. It is a jolly affair. She takes me to 'St John', very much an 'In place', but most convivial. I return to the Wellington by four o'clock and stay with Linda until about nine. The Friday discharge seems probable.

Wednesday 3 December

I take a day off from visiting. Ros was planning to go but had to pull out at the last minute because of work. Linda does not appear to mind and I suspect rather enjoys a day more or less to herself (not that Ros would have been unwelcome). Helen and Jamie visit in the evening.

Thursday 4 December

Arrive at the hospital at eleven forty after a meeting at Sunbury. Linda is in good form. I accompany her as she takes a walk down two flights of stairs looking out at different views from the one from her room and then we return by another staircase. She is beginning to yearn for home. One more night. Then I really have to start working. Not having her at home is very dull but looking after myself for a few days is not particularly taxing. When I have to look after the two of us (Helen is capable of fending for herself) then my work will be cut out. I just hope Linda can advise me – that's all, she does not have to lift a finger, just tell me what she wants and how I should do it!

For lunch I go to the Queen Anne for the last time. Two pints of 'London Pride' and an excellent 'Bangers and Mash'. Heaven.

Before I leave Linda tries on the loose-ish trousers she plans to wear tomorrow. I notice that there is a bit of pus around one of the staples in the scar and I mention to Susan, the NZ nurse on my way out. *(I'm less squeamish than I used to be so I can bear to look closely at such things and see if there is anything which does not look quite right. It helps if you can look at these things, to get used to them)* When I get home I phone Linda and she has had that staple removed. No pain! Quite straightforward. I have made an appointment for Linda to have the remainder of the staples removed on Tuesday 9 December at the Datchet surgery. We need to take a staple remover with us just in case Kathy has not got one. My tool box pliers are probably not suitable.

Friday 5 December

Out into the big wide world again

I arrive at the Wellington around ten o'clock and transfer Linda's belongings and flowers (four bouquets and five basket arrangements) to the car while she says farewell to the nurses. We return to Datchet just after eleven – the round trip including loading taking under two hours. Not bad considering the freezing fog around Denham which had barely lifted by the time we passed through on the homeward journey.

Dave and Bea pop over in the evening and bring Linda's tapestry, framed by Anthony, giving the finished article to her as a gift. Very kind.

Saturday 6 December

Dinner at the Emmans'

Linda's first outing since before her operation but still amazingly only eight days since she was under the knife. A very pleasant evening with the Balfours and Sylvia also there. Linda departs before me but I leave not particularly long after her. I am also feeling the intense tiredness you get when long term stress is eventually relieved. It will be some months before we can seriously think about a holiday but we are both going to need one. Of that I have little doubt.

Monday 8 December

I go out shopping during which time I suspect Linda does too much. Like removing heavy casseroles from inaccessible places in cupboards. The result is that she starts to bleed, or at least she notices the return of slight spotting after several days without. I don't think it is anything to worry about but I stress that she must be careful.

Tuesday 9 December

Without a stitch

We walk across to the Datchet surgery where Kathy removes the remaining twenty seven staples, debating while she does so whether or not to leave half in for another day. I think Linda would feel more confident if that were done but on balance I consider it would be better to remove the lot. They have been in eleven days and the sooner they are removed now the quicker the residual sore bits will heal. Kathy removes the lot, probably taking longer over the process than the entire operation! Not quite. She is very interested in Linda's experiences since she – Kathy – originally suggested that the pains were back related which resulted in Linda booking several sessions with a chiropracter back in June/ July. The sad news is that Linda must not bath until the weekend to allow the holes left by the staples to close over. Linda mentions the bleeding and Kathy says that provided it is not bright red and/or copious and is odourless it is probably as we suspect, old blood finding its way out. She confirms this with one of the GPs while we are there just to be absolutely safe.

BACK TO THE OLD ROUTINE

Wednesday 10 December

Back on the Taxol

To make absolutely sure that Linda does not regain her full strength too quickly I take her along for her fourth session of chemotherapy. It goes much as before although Lorraine uses an electronic meter to regulate the speed of the drip. It takes a bit of setting up until she has cleaned the mechanical parts. Even then it proves slightly temperamental. Lorraine checks Linda's scar and says that is healing well and that there is no need to wait to have a bath. We depart a little later than on previous occasions but manage to get home in time for Countdown. Four down. Two to go.

Thursday 11 December

Old Lags Lunch

Trevor drives down – without Elaine – and he and I go up to Victoria for a fairly liquid session of the BP Old Lags. Dave Crawley is there and it seems that Jan Crawley had something similar to Linda. I think she died about a year after her illness started but I didn't like to press Dave for details so I can't quite make out what treatment she had, if any. Apparently her CA 125 went absolutely berserk but whether she had chemo (and if so, what type) and/or surgery is not clear. I suspect diagnosis may have taken a long time but it is all rather academic and pointless trying to draw comparisons and distinctions between two different cases.

Weekend 12-14 December

Not at her best

We take things fairly easily as the effects of the chemo on top of post-operative weakness hits Linda rather harder than after any of the first three pre-op chemo sessions. She feels tired and sore and although she accompanies me on the Sunday to a lunch time drink at Rod and Val Lord's she is happy to leave after about an hour. Later that day she becomes alarmed as the bleeding and discharge increase. It is still probably nothing to worry about and although we are both concerned we conclude that there is little point in seeking urgent medical attention unless the blood were to appear fresh – which it doesn't.

Monday 15 December

I make an appointment with Dr Dalton for 1215. He reassures Linda that the discharge is still to be expected and could go on for up to two months. He signs Linda off until the end of January and renews her prescriptions. That evening Helen's boyfriend Jamie takes us to see some amazing Christmas lights decorating various houses in Slough and Langley. One has a tableau with Teletubbies on top of the garage and what must be close on a full-size Father Christmas climbing into the chimney. Other houses are brilliantly lit with hundreds if not thousands of lights.

Linda asks me to buy some absorbent pads so I put them on my shopping list. Fascinating objects. They are coded on the packaging according to how much flow is to be absorbed: one, two, three or four rain drop symbols – and how thick the padding – which varies from 2mm (Ultra) to 8mm (Standard/ Plus), with an intermediate 6mm which described as Goodnight. Some even have wings. Decisions, decisions. I go for two drops, Ultra, with wings. On inspection they turn out to be immense padded structures which, when dry, could probably double up as duvets.

Christmas 1997

Linda makes progress and I make Gravad Lax – from a Michael Barry recipe (much better than the pre-packed stuff – and cheaper). I do most of the cooking over the period including lunch for seven (L, Father, Win, Edward, Nicola, Helen and myself) on Christmas Day. I don't have a great deal of assistance – Linda is under strict orders to take things easy – and in fact I manage pretty well. The veggies are all prepared the day before and on the day everything goes like clockwork. Even the clearing up from the lunch is out of the way in record time. Linda, Edward, Nicola and I go for a stroll down to the river. Jamie joins us late afternoon. Edward and Nicola go to Nicola's parents for the evening and are later joined by Helen and Jamie. Before they go, Helen drives me and Win back to Garrick House. I strain my neck, shoulders and back manoeuvring Win in and out of the car. I just don't seem to get the knack of it – she isn't heavy. I think it's probably that she doesn't feel confident in my supporting her and that makes it more difficult to move her.

On Boxing Day Linda and I go to John and Annie's for brunch – smoked salmon and tasty nibbles and champagne (can't drink much as I'm driving).

I take Father back to Solihull on Saturday 27. Jamie and Helen in the meantime drive down to Dorchester, so Linda and I have the remainder of the weekend to ourselves.

We go for a short walk – in fact the longest Linda has done since her op – in Langley Park.

New Years Eve

What a way to see the year out

Chemo session number five. Same procedure as before. We arrive around ten o'clock and I leave Linda in Lorraine's hands while I head off to King Edward VII to book an Ultra Sound scan on my bladder and to do some shopping for the evening meal. I return to PMH about an hour later and Linda is about to be coupled up to the Taxol.

Helen and Jamie visit after lunch – or at least after our lunch. They munch their own food before disappearing to visit 'Tone' – in Wexham Park following his emergency appendectomy.

Hilary Thomas drops in around half past two and puts forward a proposal for Linda – and me, I suppose – to consider after the final chemo. Would she be interested in joining a clinical trial on a new chemical which in theory has been designed to envelop any remaining tumour and render it inactive, unable to fragment and create new troublesome molecules? Assuming she is interested – and no decision is required at this stage – Mr McIndoe would carry out a laparoscopy (not too drastic) to determine if any tumour is still visibly remaining. If it were, then Linda would have further treatment but would be ineligible for the trial. Provided she is clear her name would then be added to a list of around 120 volunteers from whom 1/3 are picked at random for the 'magic bullet'. The remaining two thirds are the control group. Apparently trials to date have indicated dramatically increased remission, almost approaching what could be considered to be a cure.

I think Linda is keen to volunteer – and I am in full agreement. Anything which improves the long term probability is worth doing in my view.

I think also we are both a bit sobered by the clear acknowledgement that the thing could rear its ugly head again at some stage. According to Hilary Thomas, if it reappears it is most commonly in the pelvic area, in a similar way to when it first presented itself. So removal of the ovaries etc., does not guarantee that everything has been removed. We both knew that but we have to face the possibility that it could return and that further treatment may be necessary. We will tackle that if and when it happens but in the meantime participation in the clinical trial could be of direct (if she is drawn) or indirect (if she is not) benefit.

The evening and morning of New Year 1998 are spent at Eddy and Janet's. Andrew and Margaret also go, but separately as they are not staying overnight. Linda stays up until A & M leave and the rest of us go to bed. She does not sleep too well, in part because of the affect of the chemo (it tends to make her restless for the first night or so) and partly – so she alleges – due to my snoring.

Weekend 3-5 January 1997

Linda feels a bit under the weather. Aches and pains, general fatigue, and numbness in the fingers and toes. Just the usual post-chemo effects. They are probably worse this time but she always expected a worsening of the effects as the treatment progressed. At least there is only one more to go.

Wednesday 7 January

Hair today?

Linda thinks she can feel new hair growth on her scalp. I spend some time looking in different lights and from different angles. Yes, I think there is something there but it is not very easy to see.

Saturday 10 January

Much more convinced about the hair growth today. Looks darkish but again it is difficult to tell as it is only a millimetre or so long.

A very muddy walk around the Wraysbury gravel pits on an unbelievably warm and sunny morning. Lots of birders out. Linda's longest walk for some time.

Wednesday 14 January

All clear

Linda's first check-up with Mr McIndoe since the de-bulking. We leave Datchet on the 0916 train and head initially for Knightsbridge. As Linda's appointment is not until 1245 we decided to go carpet spotting in Harrod's sale. We find something we like, open an account and put a deposit down in order to secure a 10% discount over and above the sale reduction. Off to Harley Street.

Mr McIndoe looks very cheerful and reiterates the positive comments he made following the surgery. He actually says that Linda's prognosis is good. Quite a contrast with the rather gloomy caution he expressed at the initial consultation. He examines Linda and applies silver nitrate to the top of the vagina where a small part of the wound has not completely healed. He says that it may be necessary to repeat the procedure but that it is nothing untoward. Linda asks if it is OK for us to have intercourse and he states that it would certainly do no harm and in fact may be beneficial. I say "Told you so" and we all laugh.

Off to a pub near Oxford Street where Linda and I share a bottle of red wine to celebrate her encouraging progress. She has an awful headache on the homeward journey.

During the evening Linda comments that she is discharging. Sure enough there is a fair amount of sludgy mucous which I guess is a direct result of the application of the silver nitrate. She puts one of her absorbent duvet pads in her drawers and has to change it several times, during the next day.

Friday 16 January

Breaking the fast

The sludgy discharge has now virtually ceased and we have our first intercourse, and Linda her first orgasm, since 27 November. Few problems, apart from a slight pink coloration but no discomfort.

Linda has to fast from breakfast, drinking only a litre or so of water around 1 o'clock, to prepare for an Ultra-Sound Scan of the pelvic area. Hilary Thomas likes to have one done at this stage.

We go to PMH and while I park Linda goes off to have the scan. By the time I have settled down in the reception area and am starting to mark Earthwatch applications Linda reappears. Although the formal report will be sent to Hilary in time for next Wednesday's chemo the radiologist confirms that the scan is clear.

Wednesday 21 January

Sixth and Last

I drop Linda off at PMH and then rush back home to await the new washing machine. As I arrive the phone is ringing. It is Curry's delivery to confirm that the machine will be delivered between one o'clock and five. I dash straight back to the hospital where Linda is under the care of Staff Nurse Alice as

Lorraine is on holiday. The blood count for the day is good, having risen from the low(ish) levels of the past few weeks. Last week's CA 125 is 8.8 (having fallen further, although not much) but the carcino-embryonic antigen (CEA) level is up from its usual level of around 0.1, to 3.3, which is marginally above the normal range of 0.1-3.0. Unfortunately, Hilary Thomas will not be in today as she is in Paris at a meeting so we have no chance to discover what the significance is, if any.

I leave Linda again to go home and await the washing machine. By three o'clock it has not arrived so I contact Linda to find out her progress. She is nearly finished so I suggest she hires a taxi unless the machine is delivered within the next few minutes. Apparently Hilary Thomas **is** in today and she tells Linda to disregard the CEA level (she does not recall asking for it to be monitored) unless it rises above ten! HT will get her colleague Chris Nicholson to get in touch with Linda regarding the trial.

Tuesday 27 January

"I feel really grumpy today"

The post-chemo effects really seem to get Linda down today. Aching ankles, sound echoing in her head, 'spongy' teeth, the numb fingers and feet, the irregular heart beat, all conspire to make her feel particularly low, although she recognises that this is the last time she will have to go through this phase. When Helen asks how she is, she replies that she has felt grumpy all day.

Thursday 29 January

I use our Air Miles and make a booking to go to Madrid at the end of March. That's something to look forward to.

Weekend 30 January – 1 February

It's falling out again.

We spend most of Friday and Saturday at Chris and Kate Bullen's partly on business – Helen comes with us to gain some idea of Chris's media interests- but largely and most enjoyably for pleasure. During Sunday Linda announces that she seems to be losing some of what little replacement hair has so far grown. Even so there are tantalising glimpses of yet more fine stubble. I guess she will have to be patient. It will grow. It will.

She also has a sore throat and a persistent pain in the right lower abdomen which must be causing her some concern. She complains at one point that she doesn't get the chance to have a little weep occasionally, something she feels would do her good. I am sure it would. I find myself feeling a bit helpless to think after all we've gone through she still feels that I inhibit her from letting her emotions run their course.

STARDOM AND TRIALS

Monday 2 February

Arranging the trial.

Linda leaves a message with Hilary Thomas's secretary to try to set things in motion for the clinical trial. While Linda is out a Dr Nicholson phones and he takes me through the likely course of events. He will brief his nurse (Nurse Clare Wurr) to make contact and arrange to see Linda at The Hammersmith within the next week or so. A laparoscopy will be arranged, hopefully before the end of the month and if Linda is free from visible signs of tumour she will enter the trial there and then while still under anaesthetic. If then she is in the test group the drug plus radioactive tracer will be introduced into the peritoneal cavity and she will spend an extra night in hospital while the radiation level reduces. If she is in the control group she will be allowed home the following day. In either case she will then be monitored regularly.

According to Dr Nicholson if there are visible signs of residual tumour no treatment is given at that stage. Apparently there is debate currently over whether or not further chemotherapy is necessary or effective.

Tuesday 10 February

Movie stars!

We take part in a video which is being put together by the ovarian cancer support group 'Ovacome'. It is introduced by Jenny Agutter who is the group's patron. This all came about because I contacted 'Ovacome' to see if they might be interested in this journal. We have a most enjoyable day watching Jenny Agutter do her bit (what will be no more than five to ten minutes takes several hours to get right) and then we are interviewed for our contribution. That is far quicker. Three other ovarian cancer patients – including Debbie Howells the wife of Tottenham Hotspur footballer David Howells – are also involved. It will be interesting to see how much is retained from our interview when it is finally produced. Linda is fine but I burble rather. We chat to Jenny Agutter who is warm and friendly and genuinely interested in our experiences.

Wednesday 12 February

"We are not allowed to give out results."

I take Linda for her routine blood test and while waiting ask for the previous CA 125 result. There is an awkward pause before the pathology administrator tells us that they are not allowed to divulge such information directly to the patient. We try to contact Lorraine but she is nowhere to be found. Eventually after trying to reach her by phone after we return home she calls us from her home where she is suffering from flu. Naturally she does not have the data to hand but confirms that the level continues to fall. Surely the pathology laboratory could at least have said that.

Saturday 14 February

Summer has arrived!

We spend St Valentine's Day tidying the garden. It is a most glorious sunny day and we have lunch on the patio – as we had done the day before. Today it is even warmer and Linda does her first gardening for many months without suffering too many ill effects, although she is conscious of the niggly pain in her lower abdomen.

The two of us eat at home. I prepare the starter and Linda the main course – both from dear old Delia.

Sunday 15 February

Exercise time

Yet another first for Linda. She gets up before we have our tea in bed and does twenty four minutes level one toning and aerobics exercise from her video.

Thursday 19 February
Talking about trials
We go to see one of Hilary Thomas's Research Assistants, Clare Wurr at the Hammersmith to find out more about the new cancer drug trial.

Clare is late twenties and pretty switched on. She explains that following a satisfactory – ie <23 – CA 125 (she will arrange up-to-date measurements at the Charing Cross Hospital on blood samples she removes there and then) Linda will have the laparoscopy to establish her eligibility for the trial (ie no visible signs of tumour). If she is eligible **and** is one of those selected for the trial (which is decided while she is under the anaesthetic) she will wake to find a drip tube already inserted in her abdomen ready to take around one litre of the active solution which would be freshly blended. If she wakes up to find no tube (the odds are there will **not** be one) she will have to wait a while to find out whether it is because she is simply one of the control group (the more likely reason) or if it is because residual tumour has been observed. With respect to the latter eventuality we ask the inevitable "What if?" The short answer is that nothing would be done in the short term. It seems that premature administration of further chemo is not particularly effective and it is preferable to take such action only when/if symptoms become intolerable.

In the more likely event that she is one of the control group she would be able to return home that day or perhaps the following day. She will then be checked after one month and six months.

If she receives the trial material (which is in the form of an antibody to which a low level of radioactivity has been bonded – yttrium-90-HMFG1 antibody) she will need to stay in the hospital for 48 hours. After treatment she will be seen every week for six weeks for blood tests and to check for side effects. These include skin rash and/or aching joints which generally appear after a couple of weeks. Hair loss is not an effect!

The idea behind the treatment is that the antibody attaches itself to any remaining tumour cells and the radiation destroys them. In a way it is like a very precisely targeted radio-therapy.

Clare says that in the event that laparoscopy reveals visible tumour cells it can be a problem to come to terms with taking no further action until the situation worsens. I wonder how Linda feels about that prospect.

February/March

Challenging the follicles

Linda's hair begins to grow noticeably. By early March she has a covering about 1cm long on her head. At first they were all silver but now darker ones are joining the rest. I think she looks great but she is too self conscious to go out without the wig yet. Hopefully by the time we go to Madrid she will feel more confident.

The hair is also growing under her arms, around her genitals, on her legs and her eyebrows are beginning to re-emerge.

Tuesday 10 March

All clear and under control.

It is trial day – or not as the case may be. We set off before eight o'clock for the Hammersmith Hospital to arrive for a nine o'clock admission. The traffic on the A40 around Park Royal is grim but we arrive only a few minutes late. Despite some doubts on our behalf to the contrary the arrival time appears to be correct. Linda is asked the usual string of questions by doctor/nurse/anaesthetist. The procedure is explained again. She will have a laparoscopy to establish whether or not there is any signs of disease. If there is then biopsy samples will be taken and analysed and she will not be eligible for the trial drug. If she is clear a telephone call will be made from the theatre to determine if she is subject or control. We are then told that the theatre schedule has been revised. As a result Linda is taken down to her tryst with Mr McIndoe at ten o'clock, some three and a half hours earlier than we expected. She returns at 1125 by which time I have begun to worry that something unpleasant has been discovered. But no, the good news is that she is still visibly clear of any cancer. Mr McIndoe checked out the area where Linda has been feeling discomfort when she gets tired but could see nothing untoward. So while she is eligible for the trial she unfortunately falls into the control group rather than receiving the wonder drug. A bit of an anticlimax in that respect but it is good to know that all is clear inside. We are free to depart at around half past three.

Before being formally advised that she can leave Linda has a visit from Clare Wurr and one of HT's other colleagues (missed her name I'm afraid). They confirm the outcome of the diagnosis and the selection process. Clare tells Linda that the CA 125 which was measured at the Charing Cross Hospital prior to her admission was around 8. Higher than PMH results but perfectly acceptable. Officially she is now 'in remission'.

THE "C" WORD

Saturday 28 March – Tuesday 31 March

Hola!

Our first trip abroad since Brussels last July and our first flight since January last year. We take advantage of our Air Miles and a special half points offer to fly to Madrid. We are taken out to dinner on Saturday evening by Pepe Herrero and his wife Marisol. We have a very pleasant meal and get to bed around one o'clock local time (effectively two o'clock as Spanish time (CET) moves forward one hour at the same time as BST begins.) On the Sunday, as it is raining hard, we visit the Thyssen-Bornemisza art collection before collapsing in a restaurant for a lunch. We pig ourselves rather and unfortunately after we return to the hotel for a siesta Linda is suddenly violently sick and has diarrhoea. Whether it was something we had at lunch time – we both had the same to eat – or something she ate earlier it is impossible to tell, but it is almost certainly food related.

Linda spends the evening in and out of bed while I go out for a meal. By the middle of the following morning the more unpleasant symptoms have eased and she feels strong enough to venture out into the warm spring sunshine. We spend a very pleasant couple of hours pottering in the Parque del Retiro and then in the Jardín Botánico. Linda 'comes out' for the first time and removes her wig. She leaves it off even when we go for lunch in a little bar where we have a mixture of tapas – or at least I do. Linda nibbles cautiously on a cheese baguette while I gorge myself as usual.

Linda tells me later that she had stomach pains before, during, and immediately after her bout of sickness which were not dissimilar to those she had in the early stages of her troubles. However they quickly subside so are most likely to have been associated with the gastric upset rather than being any too sinister. It just demonstrates though how sensitive she is – we both are – to the underlying threat that 'something' might return.

On our final evening we have a drink in Plaza Mayor and watch the world passing by as the sun goes down, before stopping in a small restaurant nearby for dinner. Again Linda's appetite is suitably modest but she enjoys what she has.

We return to Datchet during Tuesday afternoon. Apart from the tummy upset we have enjoyed the break and now look forward to the rather more adventurous holiday we have booked in Turkey in June.

Wednesday 1 April

Yet another test.

Linda goes to PMH for a blood sample to be taken for another Ca 125 measurement in preparation for her check up with HT next week. Six days to wonder and worry that it might have suddenly increased.

Tuesday 7 April

Good work, Professor T!

We are both a bit twitchy today. Linda admits as much to her boss on the phone but she hasn't actually said anything to me. In fact I have been feeling quite tense for some days now.

We both go in to see HT at the PMH. She is very pleased with Linda's progress – last Wednesday's CA 125 was around 8 (she has not got Linda full notes with her) – but more significantly she comments on the laparoscopy observations and the cytology associated with it. We already knew that visually all was clear but subsequent analysis of washings revealed nothing untoward. HT even uses the 'C' word (C-U-R-E). True, it is said with a fair degree of circumspection, but there does seem to be a possibility in Linda's case that we may eventually be able to speak of 'cure' rather than 'remission'.

HT also tells us she has been appointed to the Chair of Oncology at University of Guildford. Well done, Professor T! And well done, Linda!

Linda is booked in for another appointment in July.

Wednesday 8 April

Linda takes the plunge

We meet with Helen and Bob Warren for lunch at The Union. Linda leaves the wig off for the first time in public (apart from in Madrid which didn't really count). Apart from the nape of the neck where the hair is a little thinner at the moment the rest looks great. I never thought I'd fancy a woman with short grey hair but it really suits her and I hope she will have the confidence from now on to leave the wig off all the time. I am sure her hair will continue to grow even quicker without it.

Monday 20 April

Progress report

Linda's hair continues to grow vigorously. There is much dark – black? – hair on her head growing beneath the earlier silver hair. It will be interesting to see how it develops. Today she has gone off to work without the wig for the first time and this probably is the point when she abandons it altogether, so rarely has she worn it over the last couple of weeks. Overall she is feeling well with only occasional abdominal discomfort. We were rather saddened last night at news of the death of Linda McCartney whose cancer had returned suddenly, more than two years after she had breast cancer. I know what is going through both our minds but we must stay positive and live our lives as normally as we can.

Monday 11 May

Back on Court

Some months ago while she was still undergoing chemo Linda expressed the need for some goal, something to focus on. I suggested that she should aim to take up the game again within the year from having had to stop. Well, this evening she has made it. 52 weeks since she last played she met up with Richard and Caroline at their house and went on to the Ascot club to play. She managed three games, winning two of them. She is feeling very pleased and admits that until a few weeks ago she did not really think she would achieve her goal. But she has and I am also very proud of her.

Monday 18 May

Cause for concern?

When we wake up this morning Linda tells me that she has a pain in her abdomen. She noticed it when she went to the loo during the night and it has not gone away. She describes it as 'a bit like stitch.' Probably it is nothing to worry about but I cannot help but feel concerned when she gets things like this. When I contact her during the day she feels it unlikely that she will play badminton in the evening. However when she arrives home from work we knock the shuttle about on the lawn and she decides to play. In the event she plays five games, winning two. The pain appears to be subsiding.

Friday 12 June

Two days to go

We are both looking forward to our first major holiday for over a year. Linda's abdominal discomfort has vanished but she now has a pain in her right shoulder. She maintains it feels different from the shoulder pain of last year which heralded her illness. Once again though I find it difficult to put it out of my mind. This is one of the problems with being 'on the outside'. Linda can feel the pain, form a view of it – right or wrong – but I can only observe. And fret.

Sunday 14 June to Sunday 28 June

A wonderful holiday

Our two weeks in Kalkan make one of the best holidays we have had for many a year. OK, the Nile cruise was special but Kalkan was rather more relaxing and exactly what was needed after all the traumas. Unfortunately Linda's shoulder pain does not improve despite trying anti-inflammatory tablets, massage (by me) and swimming. If anything swimming makes it feel worse. Linda does not seem unduly bothered but suggests that she makes an appointment with the chiropractor when we return home.

Monday 29 June

Radio star

I accompany Linda to a recording studio near Kings Cross where she takes part in several radio links across the country. Jenny Agutter, in her capacity as Patron of Ovacome, fronts each link up with information about Ovacome and ovarian cancer. Linda and Debbie Howells alternately sit in with Jenny and answer questions about their own experiences. Linda was very nervous before the event but she speaks clearly and articulately and I think she rather enjoys the experience.

Thursday 2 July

Appointment with the chiropractor

Linda visits Rob Brydges who treated her shoulder and back last year in the early days when we thought her pains might have some association with neck or spine. He believes that her pains this time are a result of the damage caused by the cytotoxins, and as well as proceeding with massage and manipulation, he recommends Linda has a chat with their homeopathic specialist.

Wednesday 15 July

Yet another needle

For the first time in several months Linda goes to The Princess Margaret Hospital to have a blood sample taken prior to her three monthly check up with Hilary Thomas. This is the bit neither of us want to think about but I am sure we will both be on tenterhooks until next week.

Tuesday 21 July

But in your case ...

Linda looks great and is feeling well but today is check up day and the result of that blood test should be known. It is impossible not to be apprehensive about the CA 125 level – whatever its significance, and no matter how well Linda feels. It will be a disappointment if it shows a clear indication of increasing again. In the event Hilary Thomas announces the result before anything else is discussed. It is 3.6 – the lowest level Linda has recorded. It is even at the lower end of the 'normal' distribution. Following on from that encouraging piece of news Hilary alludes to the potential recurrence of the disease which is, we know, statistically more likely that not with ovarian cancer. She adds, "But in your case ..." which seems to imply once more that in Linda's case the prognosis puts her into the statistical minority. The rest of the examination proceeds smoothly and Hilary asks to see Linda again in four months time.

We duly celebrate the outcome of the check up with a meal in Windsor at Punters Wine Bar. Very pleasant.

FULL CIRCLE

Saturday 15 August

As I sit typing this entry to the journal I cannot but help reflect on how I felt one year ago from this day. Linda had just been diagnosed as having 'cancer'. At that stage neither she nor I – nor surgeon nor physician – knew precisely what type of cancer she was inflicted with. We have learned much since.

We have learned a lot about her disease, ovarian cancer. We have learned about the prognosis for the majority of women suffering the disease.

One view might be that the general prognosis is not wildly encouraging – that less than a third survive beyond five years. Another view might be that although that is a minority it is a large minority and the survival rate will improve with better awareness of the disease and prompter diagnosis and treatment.

In our (blissful) ignorance of what the future holds that latter view is the one which in our own individual ways we both hold on to. As we – and it is a shared experience – enter this new year, it is with hope rather than with trepidation that we look forward to our future together.

My part of this journal is all but finished. There is no way of telling how the story might end. It would be dishonest to claim that I do not have frequent bursts of angst. I am prone to imagine the worst in every ache or pain that Linda appears to have. This is probably natural but it can be stressful. I do however want her to be open and not to conceal things.

When I look at her today – one year on – I can only marvel at how well she coped with what she has been through, at how well she looks, and at how determined she is to continue the fight if the enemy returns.

POSTSCRIPT

2 June 1999

It is now over two years since Linda experienced the first rumblings that something insidious was lurking in the complex biochemistry of her cells. And we are approaching the second anniversary of the day of diagnosis when ovarian cancer entered our lives.

We originally called a halt to this record of Linda's illness, and the way it affected our lives, back in August 1998. However we find ourselves on the eve of publication nearly another year on and we feel an update on Linda's state of health, virtually as we go to press, is appropriate.

Today in fact is regular check up day. We go to see Professor Thomas in her new surroundings at the Guildford Nuffield. The interval between consultations is nominally four months but somehow the gap has stretched to five months or more. The longer the better. We hope there will come a day when it will be considered necessary to see Linda only once a year. We both get a bit tense in the run up to each appointment. In the absence of any worrying aches and pains all thoughts focus on the blood test result. What is the CA 125 count going to be? Today it is 5.4. A whisker up on the January figure but a change of no significance. Next appointment November.

Linda says – Two years ago I was feeling absolutely dreadful. Now I feel fine. I am still working, gardening and playing badminton regularly. However, it's impossible not to wonder from time to time if there is anything nasty going on inside me without any symptoms, giving no clues. A low CA 125 count is a great boost. Until we get close to the next check-up I can stop worrying about my mortality and concentrate on living.

Roy says – Linda looks particularly fit and tanned after two wonderful weeks in Tobago. Inevitably her illness has changed our lives in some ways. We tend to be more decisive nowadays. Whereas we might have at one time said something like 'I'd love to go to Venice, one day,' and then done nothing about it, our attitude is now 'Let's go ahead and do it.'

The possibility that the illness may return will always be at the back of our minds and I think I probably dwell on it more than Linda. But another year has passed, we are having some great times and we have too much to do together to allow that possibility to intrude. Life is good.